Contents

Chairman's Foreword

The Background

We have found that people are staggered when one confronts them with the basic facts about literacy and numeracy, and rightly so. It is staggering that over the years millions of children have been leaving school hardly able to read and write, and that today millions of adults have the same problems. Of course, one can argue about definitions, but the stark facts are all too clear. Roughly 20% of adults – that is perhaps as many as 7 million people – have more or less severe problems with basic skills, in particular with what is generally called 'functional literacy' and 'functional numeracy':

"the ability to read, write and speak in English, and to use mathematics at a level necessary to function at work and in society in general".

It is a shocking state of affairs in this rich country, and a sad reflection on past decades of schooling and policy priorities over the years.

Moreover, the key facts are not new. I drew attention to the literacy problems nearly a decade ago in my Presidential Address to the British Association for the Advancement of Science. Even then the facts were hardly new. Following that address, the National Commission on Education in the early '90s again emphasised the problem. Moreover, the Basic Skills Agency, in its sterling work, has repeatedly drawn attention to the issues and pointed towards potential solutions. But, as a national priority, improvements in literacy and numeracy never reached the front of the policy queue.

So it was most encouraging when the Government launched the National Strategies for Literacy and Numeracy for schools. This gives every hope that today's and future generations of children will have the right start. As a result, by 2050 it should have ceased to be a problem, and a Working Group such as ours should be unnecessary. But we are far from that, which is why the Government, as part of its plans for lifelong education, has included basic skills as a key area. This makes total sense, since command of these basic skills is a necessary step towards the higher goals of education throughout life.

Our Working Group was appointed by The Rt. Hon. David Blunkett, MP, Secretary of State for Education and Employment, in June 1998. The terms of reference he set us state clear objectives in improving the lot of the many adults whose quality of life can be enriched by enhancing their basic skills. All of us on the Working Group welcomed the Secretary of State's initiative and the opportunity it has given us to point the way towards *A Fresh Start*.

We are at pains in the Report to show how serious the consequences of poor or limited basic skills are for society, for the economy, and – always at the forefront of our thinking – for families and individuals. At their most severe, the handicaps for the individual can be devastating. I can't put this better than by quoting from the remarkable recent novel by Bernhard Schlink *'The Reader'(1997)*.

"I read the note and was filled with joy and jubilation. 'She can write, she can write!' In these years I had read everything I could lay my hands on to do with illiteracy. I knew about the helplessness in everyday activities, finding one's way or finding an address or choosing a meal in a restaurant, about how illiterates anxiously stick to prescribed patterns and familiar routines, about how much energy it takes to conceal one's inability to read and write, energy lost to actual living. Illiteracy is dependence. By finding the courage to learn to read and write, Hanna had advanced from dependence to independence, a step towards liberation."

But even when the problem is less extreme, it limits a person's chance to get a job or, if in a job, to achieve promotion and change. And it can close many doors to a full life. Indeed there can hardly be a surer way to social exclusion. Moreover hard economic issues are involved. Improving their basic skills can enable people to earn more, to spend more, to help the economy to grow faster. The benefits to industry and the economy may be hard to calculate, but they must be vast. It is a state of affairs that cannot be allowed to continue, and our Report proposes a wide-ranging approach to the challenge.

Our Approach

We propose a National Strategy – complementary to the strategies now in place for schools – which is intended to succeed in attracting potential learners into study schemes. To succeed, much will have to be done to improve what is on offer, to make study programmes more accessible, and to ensure that the quality and standards of curricula, and learning opportunities are attractive.

Not least, it will involve a vast expansion in information technology facilities available to learners. We are convinced that the use of Information and Communication Technology (ICT) is one of the most effective – and attractive – ways of enhancing one's basic skills. It points to a clear priority for Government, linked to what is already being done for schools.

It is a tough challenge. The key commitment has to be from Government and the fact that the Secretary of State set us ambitious terms of reference is the most encouraging signal. But once the Government has shown its support, and its willingness to provide the necessary resources, the implementation of what is needed will demand commitment and involvement from everyone, local authorities and institutions, business and industry, voluntary organisations, colleges and the media. All have a part to play in what must be a national and ongoing crusade. It has got to be as stirring as when the school-leaving age was to be raised to 16, and for other such major transformations. The work of our group was stimulated throughout by the feeling that we were dealing with something 'big', something that could help millions of fellow-citizens, and that now called for genuine devotion of national energy and resources. Given that determination, we believe that the problems can be solved.

I must mention some limitations in the scope of the Report. Geographically, it is limited to England. It does not cover Scotland or Northern Ireland, nor Wales, which has separate arrangements.

We have not addressed wider key skills, although, where appropriate, we discuss overlaps between literacy and numeracy on the one hand and key skills of communication and the application of number on the other. We have made proposals about the use of Information and Communication Technology (ICT) in helping basic skill programmes, a vital priority for the future. But we have not addressed the teaching of ICT skills as such. This issue – the future of ICT as a basic skill in itself – is of utmost importance, and is being considered by the National Skills Task Force.

In general we have not separated literacy and numeracy, except where they merit different strategies. Most adults who have difficulties with reading and writing are also weak in numeracy, but relatively few who are good at reading and writing turn out to have very poor numeracy.

Our top priority relates to adults below Level 1 in literacy and below Entry Level in numeracy*, which means roughly 20% of adults. This is the threshold of functional literacy and functional numeracy, although in due course most people might achieve a higher level. So we have thought it important to bear in mind what happens beyond, not least for Level 2.

Most of our proposals are appropriate for teaching English as an additional language (EAL), and certainly we have kept this in mind throughout. At certain points we refer to special EAL aspects. But it would be sensible if a separate effort is made, following this report, to review its special implications in the EAL context.

We have not been able to consider the special needs of adults with learning disabilities who wish or need to improve their basic skills. We are conscious of the important concerns at issue. In particular, there is the need to ensure that sufferers from dyslexia are helped with targeted basic skills programmes, where needed. This calls for a special study, following this report, to assess where its recommendations are appropriate and where they should be supplemented.

Our *Recommendations* are set out at the end of individual chapters (from Chapter 5 onwards) and are brought together in a single list at the end. This is followed by our proposed *Implementation Plan*, suggesting the timescale, costs and responsibility for individual recommendations.

Our Work Pattern

We started in June 1998, and met on 20 occasions. We had discussions with the main organisations involved in relevant funding and provision arrangements, including the Further Education Funding Council, the Qualifications and Curriculum Authority, the Local Government Association, the Training and Enterprise Councils National Council, the Training Standards Council, and the Office for Standards in Education. We met with Dr Thomas Sticht, a leading researcher on adult basic skills in the United States. The Minister

**See Annex A, which explains what is meant by these terms, and the measurements involved*

for Employment, Welfare to Work and Equal Opportunities, Andrew Smith, MP, addressed one of our meetings; and we were also helped by a discussion with Baroness Blackstone, the Minister for Further and Higher Education, at a Basic Skills Agency Board Meeting.

A wide range of organisations and individuals responded to our public invitation to give evidence, either in writing or via the web site: they are listed in Annex B, as are all the organisations which met with us. We held seminars with basic skills tutors and learners.

Acknowledgements

Our task deserved the commitment and urgency required by the Secretary of State. I would like to express my appreciation to members of the Working Group for their individual contributions and their collective determination to produce an effective Report. Everyone has worked hard and constructively.

We were set up as an independent Committee. But we have worked closely with the Department for Education and Employment and with the Basic Skills Agency, and especially with Mr Derek Grover, Director, Skills and Lifelong Learning and the senior representative of the Department; and with Mr Alan Wells, Director of the Basic Skills Agency, who was our specialist adviser. Both took part throughout in our discussions, and we are immensely indebted to them for bringing their experience and wisdom to our deliberations.

An enormous amount of work had to be done in producing briefing papers for the Working Group and with all the back-up a Committee such as ours needs. I want to express our thanks to Felicity Everiss, Marie Devall and Ian McVicar from the Department of Education and Employment; and to Jim Pateman, Charlotte Pearson and Jaz Bangar from the Basic Skills Agency. They have worked tirelessly and with evident effect.

I should note that a number of the key briefing papers prepared by the BSA will be issued in a separate publication.

Claus Moser

26.02.99

Working Group on Post-School Basic Skills

Terms of Reference

The Group will advise on ways in which the Government's plans for basic skills provision for adults can be supported and developed to achieve the target to help 500,000 adults a year by 2002.

The Group will identify and consider:

- the effectiveness of different kinds of provision (including that supported by FEFC, LEAs, programmes for unemployed people and other initiatives) and coordination between them;
- models of good practice in coherent delivery and funding of basic skills and ways to disseminate them;
- ways of increasing the volume, quality and effectiveness of literacy and numeracy opportunities across all learning environments.

The Group will liaise closely with the National Literacy and Numeracy Strategy Group. It will report to the Secretary of State by the end of November 1998 and provide interim advice by the end of July. In carrying out its work it will ensure that it takes full account of the roles and responsibilities of all relevant funding and providing and quality assurance bodies, and the need for value for money.

Membership of the Working Group on Post-School Basic Skills

Chairman
Sir Claus Moser KCB CBE FBA
Chairman
The Basic Skills Agency, and of The British Museum Development Trust

Members
Professor Michael Barber
Head of the Standards and Effectiveness Unit
Department for Education and Employment

Mr. Steven Broomhead
Chief Executive
Warrington Borough Council

Professor John Bynner
Director
Centre for Longitudinal Studies, Institute of Education

Mr. Mike Carnaby
Adult Learner
Sheffield Hallam University

Professor R.H. Fryer CBE
Assistant Vice-Chancellor [Lifelong Learning]
University of Southampton

Mr. Nick Henwood
Strategic Director of Education and Libraries Directorate
Kent County Council

Ms. Jean Irvine
Groupwide Customer Support Strategy Director
The Post Office

Professor Richard Layard
Director
Centre for Economic Performance, London School of Economics

Mrs. Andrea Mearing
Director of Student Services
Norfolk County Council

Sir David Nicholas CBE
Formerly Chairman,
Independent Television News

Ms. Sarah Perman
Senior Policy Officer
Trades Union Congress

Ms. Annette Zera
Principal
Tower Hamlets College

Assessor
Mr. Derek Grover CB
Director of Skills and Lifelong Learning, DfEE

Adviser
Mr. Alan Wells OBE
Director, The Basic Skills Agency

Joint Secretariat
[DfEE] Felicity Everiss, Marie Devall and Ian McVicar

[Basic Skills Agency] Jim Pateman, Charlotte Pearson and Jaz Bangar

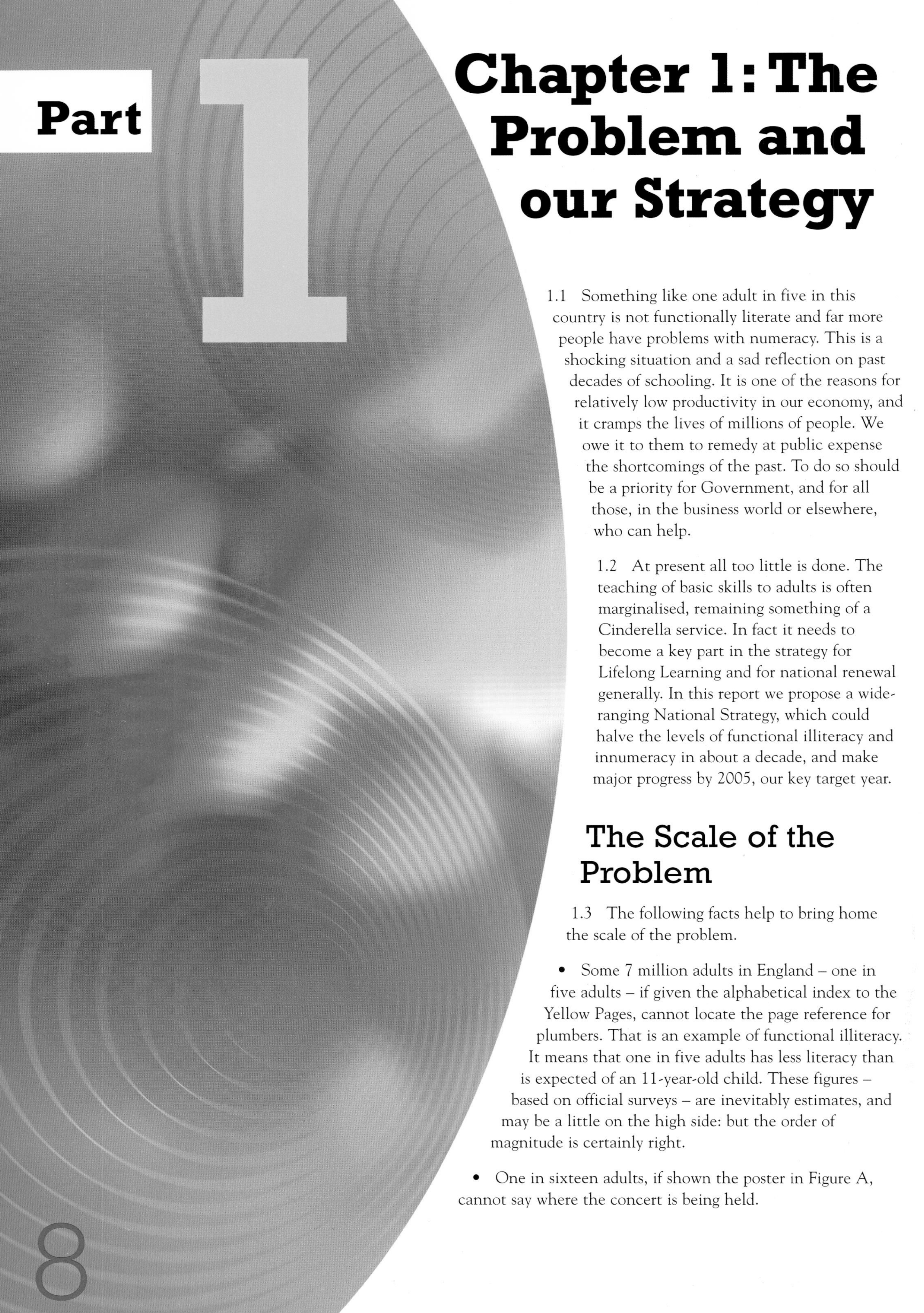

Chapter 1: The Problem and our Strategy

1.1 Something like one adult in five in this country is not functionally literate and far more people have problems with numeracy. This is a shocking situation and a sad reflection on past decades of schooling. It is one of the reasons for relatively low productivity in our economy, and it cramps the lives of millions of people. We owe it to them to remedy at public expense the shortcomings of the past. To do so should be a priority for Government, and for all those, in the business world or elsewhere, who can help.

1.2 At present all too little is done. The teaching of basic skills to adults is often marginalised, remaining something of a Cinderella service. In fact it needs to become a key part in the strategy for Lifelong Learning and for national renewal generally. In this report we propose a wide-ranging National Strategy, which could halve the levels of functional illiteracy and innumeracy in about a decade, and make major progress by 2005, our key target year.

The Scale of the Problem

1.3 The following facts help to bring home the scale of the problem.

- Some 7 million adults in England – one in five adults – if given the alphabetical index to the Yellow Pages, cannot locate the page reference for plumbers. That is an example of functional illiteracy. It means that one in five adults has less literacy than is expected of an 11-year-old child. These figures – based on official surveys – are inevitably estimates, and may be a little on the high side: but the order of magnitude is certainly right.
- One in sixteen adults, if shown the poster in Figure A, cannot say where the concert is being held.

1.4 The situation for numeracy is both worse and more confusing because the tests are weaker and the evidence is controversial. Estimates of the percentage of adults having some numeracy problems range from 30% to 50%. We regard 40% as a reasonable figure to have in mind in this report. But we also adopt a division often used (even if arbitrary) between "low" and "very low" numeracy, the latter category being those with very severe difficulties. On this basis something like one in five adults have very low numeracy. The following are survey findings about numeracy:

- one in three adults in this country cannot calculate the area of a room that is 21x14 feet, even with the aid of a calculator;
- one in four adults cannot calculate the change they should get out of £2 when they buy the goods displayed in Figure B.

1.5 What is clear from research is that very limited numeracy can be as serious as poor literacy for the individual, in certain jobs and indeed for the economy.

Figure A

THE FIRM

Appearing at the

BIRMINGHAM NATIONAL EXHIBITION CENTRE

On

19 November 1991

at

7.30pm

Tickets:
£8.50, £10.00 £15.00

Figure B

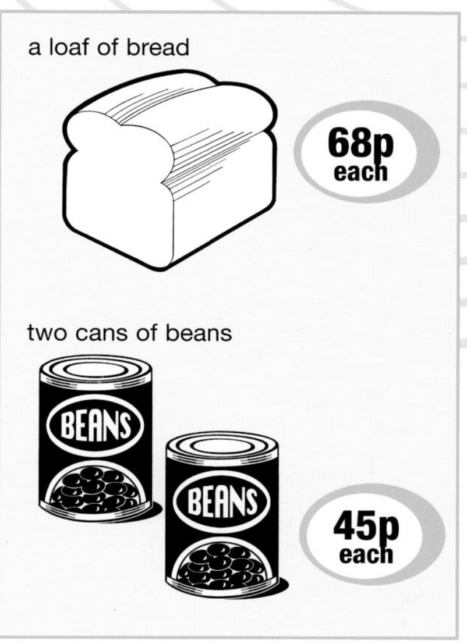

1.6 In short, for many people limited basic skills mean serious disadvantages – at work (in fact many are unemployed), and in limiting much of what a full life can offer. Limited skills are also a brake on the economy, one of the factors – as research has repeatedly shown – underlying the nation's relatively poor productivity compared with much of Europe. Table 1.1 shows some relevant comparisons*.

Table 1.1

Percentage of adults with low literacy and low numeracy (identical questions in all countries)

	Literacy	Numeracy
Germany	12%	7%
Canada	17%	17%
Britain	23%	23%

Source: *Adult Literacy in Britain*, ONS, 1997

1.7 The scale of the problem is enormous, and there is much evidence to show how it relates to other social issues. One fact will

**These figures relate to Level 1 as defined in the International Adult Literacy Survey (OECD). Definitions of levels are explained in Annex A.*

suffice to illustrate the point: some 60% of people in prison suffer from functional illiteracy and/or innumeracy.

The Causes

1.8 The situation has come about from home circumstances and, above all, from poor schooling. Certainly, a major part of the problem goes back to past education, the fact that over the years millions of children have left school with poor basic skills. Fortunately, this school problem is now being tackled through the National Strategies for Literacy and Numeracy. These reforms are crucial, but it will inevitably take decades before they have affected all the adult population. We therefore need major help in basic skills for today's adults.

1.9 Some of the provision already available for adults is excellent, with dedicated teachers and imaginative programmes. But the provision varies from area to area, in quality and in quantity: there simply is not enough provision of study programmes to meet the need. Nor has there been a coherent and consistent set of national standards to guarantee quality in what is taught, how it is taught and in the qualifications that are awarded at the end. Most of the teachers are part-time with little access to training, and the system of inspection needs coordination.

1.10 There are inevitably problems of motivation among prospective learners. Of the estimated 7 million adults who are functionally illiterate or innumerate, only about 250,000 are taking part in a relevant course of study. This is partly because people with difficulties are often understandably reluctant to acknowledge, or are unaware, that they have a problem; or that it matters or indeed that there are ways of tackling it. Moreover, few employers take a constructive approach to advancing basic skills in their workforce.

1.11 Programmes of study are insufficiently publicised, and are often not accessible enough to encourage potential learners to take part. Nor do they generally seem inviting. We attempt in this report to find a set of changes that can genuinely produce more attractive offerings for those who want to improve their basic skills.

A National Strategy

1.12 We need a Fresh Start available and attractive for millions of people. With this in mind, we propose a National Strategy for Adult Basic Skills with ten main elements.

- National targets
- An entitlement to learn
- Guidance, assessment and publicity
- Better opportunities for learning
- Quality
- A new curriculum
- A new system of qualifications
- Teacher training and improved inspection
- The benefits of new technology
- Planning of delivery

National Targets

1.13 The targets should be both ambitious and realistic. We propose that by 2010 the aim should be to reduce by half the number of functionally illiterate adults of working age. This means lifting some 3.5 million adults out of functional illiteracy over this period, and a similar number for numeracy.

A decade is a long way off, and we make recommendations for 2005 as a crucial intermediate target year, with significant improvements by then.

1.14 A key objective must be to encourage and help younger people, and we suggest that by 2010, the aim should be that 95% of 19 year olds would have adequate levels of literacy and 90% adequate levels of numeracy.

1.15 The system of provision we recommend below will make it possible to achieve the proposed targets only if each year from 2002 on average 450,000 people pass the threshold for literacy, and a similar number for numeracy. This compares with, say, less than 70,000 a year under present arrangements.

1.16 To get a flow of 450,000 people to cross the key threshold, the total number enrolled needs to increase from the 500,000 planned for 2002 to some 750,000 by 2005. The University for Industry will play an important role in this, and the targets will only be achievable if employers generally agree to play their part.

1.17 As indicated above, the targets need to have staging posts between now and a decade hence. To make sense of these targets, the Government will have to undertake a baseline survey. Then the targets will be achievable if the Government is willing to give them high priority in funding.

An Entitlement to Learn

1.18 The targets will be hard to reach unless people who want to improve their basic skills are entitled, free of charge, to all aspects of the necessary teaching and study programmes. There is already free full-time education up to 19, and – for those who qualify – highly subsidised higher education. It is only right that those who missed out early in life should have free access to acquiring the basic tools necessary for their lives.

1.19 Every citizen with worries about literacy or numeracy should have a clear entitlement to a choice of opportunities for learning, and indeed access to a wide variety of study programmes.

1.20 Individual Learning Accounts, which are part of Government programmes, can usefully be brought into play as an incentive for learners.

Guidance, Assessment and Publicity

1.21 The principle of entitlement is very important. Individuals with basic skills problems should be entitled to free confidential assessment, whether they are employed or unemployed.

1.22 All unemployed people without GCSE/O-Level, and others signing on for social benefits, should be entitled to a simple assessment test when they first sign on. If they have basic skills problems, they should be advised on appropriate courses; whether they then decide to participate is, of course, up to them.

1.23 High quality guidance and information on basic skills courses need to be freely available to all potential learners. Furthermore, to ensure that learners get on to appropriate courses, it is essential that, however they arrive there, they have had an assessment recording the skills with which they enter the programme.

1.24 Persuasive and wide-ranging publicity is important, and we are encouraged by the commitment of the BBC in this area. The recommendations we make build on this, and also set out a wide role for broadcasters and the media generally. We envisage a continuous high-profile campaign.

Better Opportunities for Learning

1.25 The scale of opportunities available to those who wish to learn needs to be enlarged. The basic problem is that courses are insufficiently intensive and there are not enough of them that offer easy access. Moreover, what is available in a particular area or institution seems quite a lottery.

1.26 Typically, basic skills learners are taught for 2-4 hours a week. For most learners, this is too little and explains why only about a third achieve their learning objectives. Research suggests that more intensive programmes increase the success rate of basic skills learners, and that longer periods of study are necessary for those with the weakest skills. We must ensure that such opportunities are widely available.

1.27 There should be a wide diversity of places and programmes in which people can access learning. All forms of provision need to be expanded, especially those that can reach adults at present felt – however wrongly – to be out of reach. Unless community–based provision is enormously expanded, we will not be able to reach hundreds of thousands of people who have real needs but don't want to go to a college. The role of voluntary organisations and community schools is crucial. All types of places – whether libraries, arts centres, supermarkets or sports centres – could be brought into play.

1.28 The New Deals have a crucial role to play in making sure that unemployed people get the opportunity to improve basic skills, and we make recommendations aimed at this role. Similarly, we know that many students in colleges of further education require additional support with basic skills in order to cope with the demands of their courses. We propose a substantial expansion in this support.

1.29 Family literacy, involving parents and children together, has proved a particularly encouraging way of helping many parents to improve their own literacy. This too needs expansion. We envisage that the Basic Skills Agency should develop its work in this area.

1.30 The most encouraging new vehicle for promoting basic skills is the University for Industry. This will use mainly interactive electronic teaching material delivered on computer screens, either on-line or by CD ROM, with guidance from a face-to-face teacher. The UfI will work through some 2,000 franchised centres throughout the country, and will also be accessed from homes and workplaces. There is funding for the UfI to support free education in basic skills for 200,000 learners by 2003.

1.31 Perhaps the most radical change relates to the key role employers have in promoting basic skills. They need to demand more skill of their employees and to do more to help their employees to acquire it. We propose a number of specific measures:

- basic skills education at the workplace should be publicly funded on the same basis as anywhere else, for example in colleges. This includes basic skills education through the University for Industry;
- a Workplace Basic Skills Development Fund should be established to provide seed funding for employers to set up basic skills programmes and to get free advice on how to organise effective basic skills courses at the workplace;
- employers wishing to gain Investors in People should have effective arrangements for diagnosing and handling problems of basic skills;
- a 'pledge' scheme for companies should be introduced so that they can indicate their support for the National Strategy;
- union representatives should be involved in the handling of basic skills issues.

1.32 A very important problem is how to ensure that busy employees have enough time for intensive study to overcome literacy, numeracy or language problems. This means that there should be adequate provision and government funding for day release.

Quality

1.33 But we need not only enough provision, but provision of such good quality that it will lift peoples' competence in a clear and demonstrable way, and be a positive attraction for students. Four elements are essential for ensuring high quality:

- clear, unambiguous national quality standards;
- a well-defined curriculum;
- a credible set of qualifications;
- a new system of teacher training and inspection.

A New Curriculum

1.34 We emphasise the need for a core curriculum that recognises the fact that different adult learners have hugely different motivations for learning. Some want it for a particular job or for work in general, others to follow a sport, to read the news, to help in working on DIY or to prepare for other forms of learning later in life. The materials through which different people learn must be addressed to their specific interests.

1.35 In all these pursuits there is a high common factor. All require the skills that are the basic building blocks of reading, writing and the use of numbers: for example comprehension, punctuation, spelling, addition, subtraction, multiplication and division. The core curriculum for adults, as for school-children, needs to cover these common elements. We propose that a basic skills curriculum, based on well-defined standards, be developed jointly by the Qualifications and Curriculum Authority (QCA), the Standards and Effectiveness Unit (SEU) and the Basic Skills Agency (BSA).

A New System of Qualifications

1.36 It is also vital that we have qualifications which are credible indicators of a person's literacy and numeracy. Unless the qualifications are credible, they cannot do the job that is needed. One of the reasons why basic skills education has not developed as it should is that so many existing qualifications lack credibility. The key criterion in planning for a new system of qualifications is that they should be attractive to potential learners, and positively useful to them in their work, in seeking and getting jobs, and in moving on to further learning.

1.37 The new system of qualifications we propose will be based on the new curriculum and on uniform standards of skill. It will be available at a number of levels, and it can be taken in 'bite-size' chunks. Ready access for the learner is crucial. Coursework-assessed qualifications, strictly based on new national standards, will be offered by a number of awarding bodies, and in addition we recommend a single test-assessed qualification at Level 1 and at Level 2, named the National Literacy Test and the National Numeracy Test. The key point is that, whatever the assessment route, it should be based on the proposed standards of curricula, teaching and so forth.

Teacher training and Inspection

1.38 Without enough good teachers there is little hope of achieving the proposed targets. At present, too many teachers teach part-time, and some are inadequately prepared. To achieve our aims, many more teachers will need to be trained to teach for the new curriculum. We shall require over 15,000 full-time equivalent teachers in this area, compared with under 4,000 at present. Teacher training programmes will have to be commensurate. And a new qualification for teachers should be developed jointly by QCA, the Further Education National Training Organisation (FENTO), the BSA and others.

1.39 Quality control also depends on proper monitoring of teaching. Basic skills education is currently in the hands of three separate inspectorates – the Further Education Funding Council Inspectorate, the Training Standards Council and OFSTED. At present the standards demanded by these bodies are insufficiently rigorous, and there should be a new common framework of inspection. This should be based on new nationally determined standards which all basic skills programmes will be required to meet to qualify for funding.

The Benefits of New Technology

1.40 Information and communications technologies (ICT) are a powerful tool in the process of raising levels of literacy and numeracy. New technology offers a new start for adults, with computers and multimedia software providing attractive ways of learning. The Web enables access to the best materials and the most exciting learning opportunities. The Internet and digital TV technology can reach into the home, to motivate and teach adults who will not join programmes in traditional centres of learning. Learners who use ICT for basic skills double the value of their study time, and acquire keyboard and other computing skills as they improve their reading, writing or use of numbers.

1.41 So ICT needs to be a staple of basic skills programmes. Learners need access to fast, modern computers. There must be an improved range of software programs suitable for these learners, with clear quality criteria for content and use. Programme providers will also need staff skilled in the best use of ICT.

Planning of Delivery

1.42 Ultimately the Government must be responsible for the achievement of the National Strategy. But this cannot be achieved without being translated into local targets and local action plans. At present local action is fragmented, partly due to the many funding sources involved. Provision in colleges is mainly financed by the Further Education Funding Council (FEFC), but there is also provision by Local Education Authorities (in institutes and community institutions) and by Training and Enterprise Councils (in colleges and private training providers). To deal with this confusion, which applies also to other forms of post-16 education and training, the Government is proposing Local Learning Partnerships. To achieve the National Strategy proposed in this report, these partnerships should have a key, indeed early, responsibility for improving adult basic skills. They should therefore be required to produce 3-year action plans for adult basic skills education. These plans should be developed with help from the Basic Skills Agency, which would also advise on the plans when submitted to the Secretary of State for approval.

1.43 At national level there should be a National Adult Basic Skills Strategy Group, chaired by a Minister, to oversee and advise on all aspects of the National Strategy. The Basic Skills Agency would continue to promote and disseminate good practice. It would also work closely with QCA and the DfEE's Standards and Effectiveness Unit in developing curricula and qualifications, and with FENTO on the training and certification of teachers.

Funding

1.44 The task is considerable and it cannot be accomplished unless the Government allocates the necessary resources. We set out in the report our best estimate of what resources might be needed – specifically by 2005 – to reduce the number of adults with poor basic skills as dramatically as we hope. Many of our recommendations are cost-neutral and quite a few do not impact on public expenditure. But of those that do, the funding called for is directly related to the increase in learners which is central to the proposed strategy. We hope that our argument for a major transformation will convince those with the power to translate it into reality.

Now is the time for a Fresh Start.

Part 2

Chapter 2: The Scale of Need

Literacy

2.1 Roughly one in five adults has low literacy skills[1]. However, it is important to emphasise that we are dealing with a spectrum of need ranging from adults who cannot read or write at all to people who may want to brush-up rusty skills. It would be naive to suggest that everyone needs or seeks the same kind of help. So we need an idea of the numbers of people at different levels of "low basic skills".*

2.2 Research by the Centre for Longitudinal Studies (CLS) for the Basic Skills Agency has divided the overall 19% with weak literacy skills into two categories[2]. About 6% of the adult working population are judged to have "very low" literacy skills; and a further 13% to have "low" literacy skills. Those with "very low" skills are likely to have great difficulty with any reading, struggling to read the simplest and shortest texts, though they may be able to cope with simple signs and advertisements, especially when these are illustrated. As an example, a sample of British-born adults were shown the poster in Figure A (shown in Chapter 1) and were asked where the concert would be held; 6% could not give the correct answer.

2.3 A further 13% (making 19% in all) of adults are defined as having "low" literacy skills. They may be able to read a short article from a tabloid newspaper and pick out favourite programmes from a TV guide, but may read slowly with little understanding. For example, the same sample of adults were given the index of the Yellow Pages and asked on which page they would find the details for plumbers; 22% were unable to answer correctly.

2.4 Identifying different groups is important because of the different needs involved. Clearly, individuals with very low skills may require different types of provision from the 13% with less serious problems. Hence our emphasis on diversity of study programmes later in the report.

As mentioned in the Summary Chapter 1, we set out in Annex A the definition of levels used in this Report.

2.5 Table 2.1 indicates the relation between the literacy problem and the Qualification and Curriculum Authority's (QCA) National Framework of Qualifications. "Very low" literacy skills means skills below Entry Level, and "low" literacy skills means achieving Entry Level, but not yet reaching Foundation Level, which is the equivalent of an NVQ Level 1.

2.6 To show how basic these levels are, Table 2.2 suggests – very broadly – how they correspond to standard levels of vocational qualifications and in the National Curriculum in schools. This means that the one in five adults with "low literacy" we refer to are below the standard norm expected of 11 year olds.

2.7 Many adults who have Foundation Level skills, have not reached the Intermediate Level of the National Framework of Qualifications; this is the level required to achieve GCSE grades A*-C. While they may have literacy problems, they can largely cope with the daily demands of reading and writing. For these adults, attainment of key skills and other qualifications at Level 2 is a more likely and appropriate goal in the context of the National Learning targets announced by the Government in 1998.

2.8 Though all countries have problems of poor literacy, Britain and the US have more severe problems than most. In 1997, the International Adult Literacy Survey (IALS) made a standard literacy assessment of 12 countries and Table 2.3 shows how poorly Britain compares with our international competitors. Of the twelve countries in the survey, only Poland and Ireland had a higher proportion at this low level than Britain.

Table 2.1: Definition and Scale of Literacy Need

Literacy Skills	Very low	Low
QCA National Framework of Qualifications Equivalent Level	Below Entry Level	Entry Level (but below Level 1)
% of adult population at this level	6	13

Source: *It Doesn't Get Any Better*, Bynner and Parsons, 1997

Table 2.2: Equivalent National Levels

QCA National Framework of Qualifications Level	Entry Level	Foundation	Intermediate
Basic Skills Agency Basic Skills Standards	Entry Level	Level 1	Level 2
Equivalent Vocational Qualifications	–	Level 1 NVQ	Level 2 NVQ
Equivalent Levels in Schools (age at which this is the norm)	2 (age 7)	4 (age 11)	GCSE A*-C (age 16)

Source: QCA

Table 2.3: Percentage of adults with literacy skills at the lowest level*

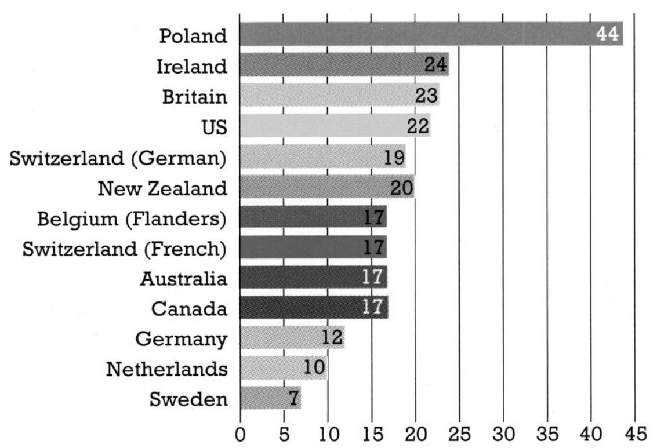

Source: *Literacy Skills for the Knowledge Society*, OECD, 1997

*These figures, and those in Table 2.5 relate to the IALS estimates for Level 1 (see Annex A).

Table 2.4 Definition and Scale of Numeracy Need

Numeracy Skills	Very poor	Poor
National Qualifications Framework Level	Below Entry Level	Entry Level
% of adult population at this level	23	25

Source: *It Doesn't Get Any Better*, Bynner and Parsons, 1997

Table 2.5: Percentage of adults with numeracy skills at the lowest level

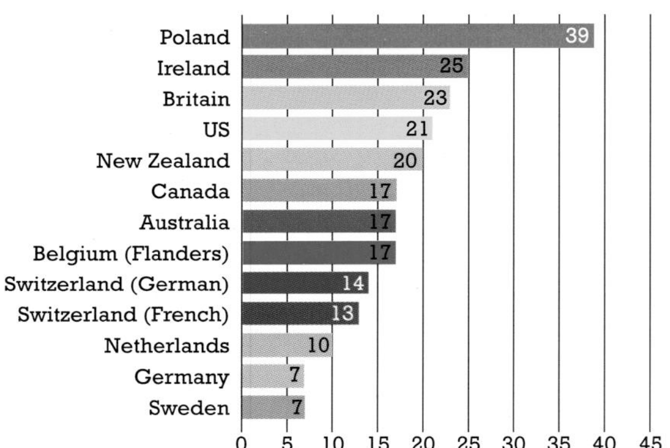

Source: *Literacy Skills for the Knowledge Society*, OECD, 1997

Table 2.6: Percentage of adults getting less than six right answers*

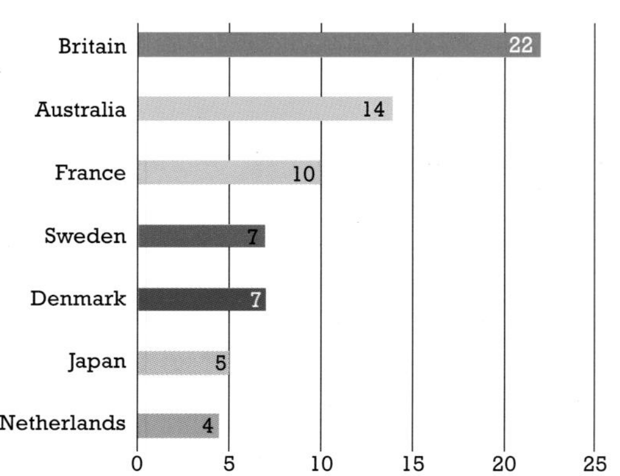

Source: *International Numeracy Survey*, The Basic Skills Agency, 1997

Numeracy

2.9 Problems with numeracy are even more common than with literacy. Some researchers suggest that nearly half of all adults in Britain have numeracy skills below the level expected of an 11 year old. A quarter are estimated to have "very low" numeracy skills, which means that they are unlikely to be able to perform even the simplest calculations. The survey carried out by the CLS asked the following question: if you bought the items in Figure B (see Chapter 1) and paid £2, how much change would you get? A quarter of respondents could not give the correct answer.

2.10 A further group of adults are judged to have what is sometimes termed "low" numeracy. These adults, while coping with the simplest transactions, would find it difficult to deal with fractions or percentages and find number manipulation a slow and arduous task. In the CLS research referred to above, when asked to work out the area of a room that was 21 ft by 14 ft, a third of all adults gave the wrong answer, even though calculators were allowed.

2.11 Table 2.4 illustrates the scale of need for numeracy, estimated by the CLS survey.

2.12 In comparison with other countries, Britain if anything does worse in numeracy than in literacy, as illustrated in Table 2.5.

2.13 The same situation emerged from a survey conducted for the Basic Skills Agency in 1996. A sample of adults in various countries were asked twelve fairly simple numeracy questions. Britain had many more people getting less than six right answers than any other country, as Table 2.6 illustrates.

The source for these figures is different from that in Table 2.3 and 2.5

2.14 We need to stress that the evidence on numeracy is less straightforward than on literacy. There are problems of definition and the tests are weaker. Even so, it is clear that a person's problems can range from almost total inability to deal with numbers to more marginal difficulties. Hence the dividing line between 'very poor' and 'poor' numeracy commented on above. Where one draws the dividing line is arbitrary. In our judgement, it is reasonable to think of some 40% of adults as having some numeracy problems, half of whom we would classify as having 'very low' numeracy. Our thoughts throughout focus on this latter category.

English Language Skills

2.15 In addition to the problems of poor literacy and numeracy, research undertaken by the Institute of Education and MORI has estimated that almost half a million people whose first language is not English have little command of the English language. As Table 2.7 shows, there are significant differences between different linguistic groups[3]. For example, of Gujerati speakers, 11% scored at the lowest level (zero score) compared to 37% of Punjabi speakers.

2.16 Overall, about one in four of the sample obtained a 'zero score', meaning that they could not:

- fill in their names and addresses
- understand a simple notice
- read their child's school timetable
- use a calendar

even when given instructions in their own language.

2.17 Nearly three-quarters of the total sample scored below 'survival' level, meaning they had difficulty completing simple forms and communicating in writing at the level of simple notes and messages. Therefore, a significant number of people from linguistic minority communities have very little knowledge or understanding of English; and a rather higher number have only limited English language skills.

Table 2.7: Language skills of linguistic minority groups (1995)

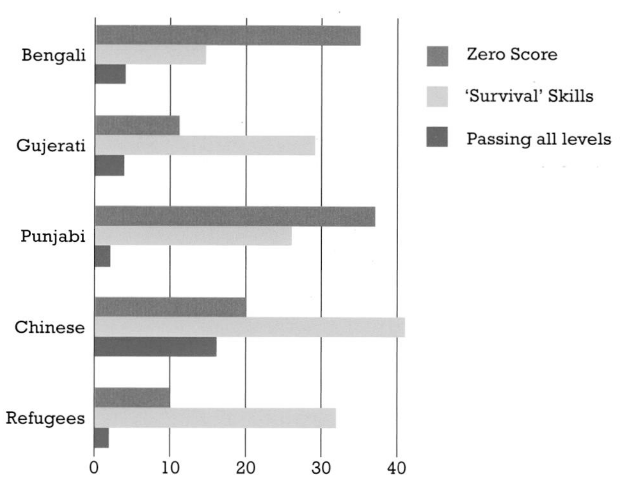

Source: Lost Opportunities: The Language skills of linguistic minorities in England and Wales,

Carr-Hill, Passingham, Wolf with Kent, The Basic Skills Agency, 1996

Basic Skills and Age

2.18 Surveys of the scale of need for literacy and numeracy skills suggest that levels of need are similar across the population between the ages of 16 and 45. However, skills problems tend to rise with people over 45. Table 2.8 shows the percentage of adults in each age group defined as being in the lowest skills category.

Table 2.8: Percentage of adults with poor literacy and numeracy by age (1997)

Age	% IALS Lowest Category Literacy	% IALS Lowest Category Numeracy
16-25	17	22
26-35	18	20
36-45	17	19
46-55	22	24
56-65	39	35
Total	**22**	**23**

Source: *Adult Literacy in Britain*, ONS, 1997

2.19 A survey of the language skills of those for whom English is not their first language[4], found a large difference between the youngest, many of whom had presumably had the benefit of schooling in English, and the older age groups. Table 2.9 illustrates this.

Table 2.9: % understanding English a little or not at all

Age	%
19-25	9
26-35	28
36-45	29
46-55	30
56+	44

Source: *A Nation's Neglect*, The Basic Skills Agency, 1989

2.20 Surveys of adult literacy and numeracy undertaken in the last 25 years have varied in their sampling methods and provide little basis for estimating trends over time. However, research by NFER[5] does suggest that over individual life-cycles, people's literacy skills do alter after they leave school, improving into early middle age, remaining steady for some time, before declining again in later years. This is supported by a longitudinal study carried out between 1961-72[6] (based on adults aged 16 in 1961 and 27 in 1972), which suggested that average literacy skills do improve during this time.

2.21 However, variations in an individual's literacy/numeracy skills over life will depend in part on the extent to which these skills are actually needed in day-to-day life. The data from the IALS survey makes clear that a decline in literacy is associated more with differing life experiences than with ageing, and that – not surprisingly – people can lose some of their reading and writing abilities if their daily life and work makes little demand on them[7]. Similarly, research carried out by CLS shows that literacy, and in particular numeracy, tend to decline during time spent out of employment, though the likelihood of decline is reduced once a threshold level of skills is reached[8].

Individual Awareness of Poor Basic Skills

2.22 The above figures come from tests of adult functional literacy and numeracy. They are in striking contrast to people's own perceptions. Various surveys have shown that many adults underestimate their need for help. Less than 5% of adults say they have a problem with reading and much the same small proportion acknowledge a difficulty with numbers. Only spelling is acknowledged as a problem by significant numbers – around 10%. Many people are unaware of their poor skills, and many, even if aware, don't regard it as a problem. And of course there is often a strong stigma in admitting to it.

2.23 In part, the lack of awareness, and perhaps of a need for improvement, reflects the low educational aspirations felt by so many. We cannot take for granted – far from it – that the importance of education and of wanting to improve one's lot, is felt by most people. This is a crucial background to our proposals. An appraisal of one's own needs will obviously effect how one can be motivated to join some kind of study programme. But, as is clear from research – for example *The Basic Skills Of Young Adults*[9] – though many people who perceive themselves as having problems do come to classes, the great majority do not. How to make it all attractive, accessible and obviously worthwhile is the key issue. Motivation – and how to encourage it – is all.

Special Needs

2.24 We are conscious of the needs of adults with learning difficulties and disabilities, some of whom certainly require help to improve their literacy and numeracy. This is a complex problem because of the range of difficulties and disabilities involved. Some, for instance, may want social and living skills more urgently than improved basic skills in the sense of this report. In considering this issue, we have taken note of the Tomlinson Report[10] . Many adults with learning difficulties have low literacy and numeracy, but their needs may demand a curriculum wider than these basic skills. The Tomlinson Report rightly argued for greater guidance and collaboration in meeting the needs of such learners, and more effective support on courses.

2.25 It is also important to note that some adults with poor literacy are dyslexic. Whilst we have not been able to give specific attention to this, we believe that much of what we recommend about effective teaching will also help dyslexic adults.

2.26 However, it is important that following this Report, special studies be undertaken relating to specific literacy and numeracy problems for people in these groups.

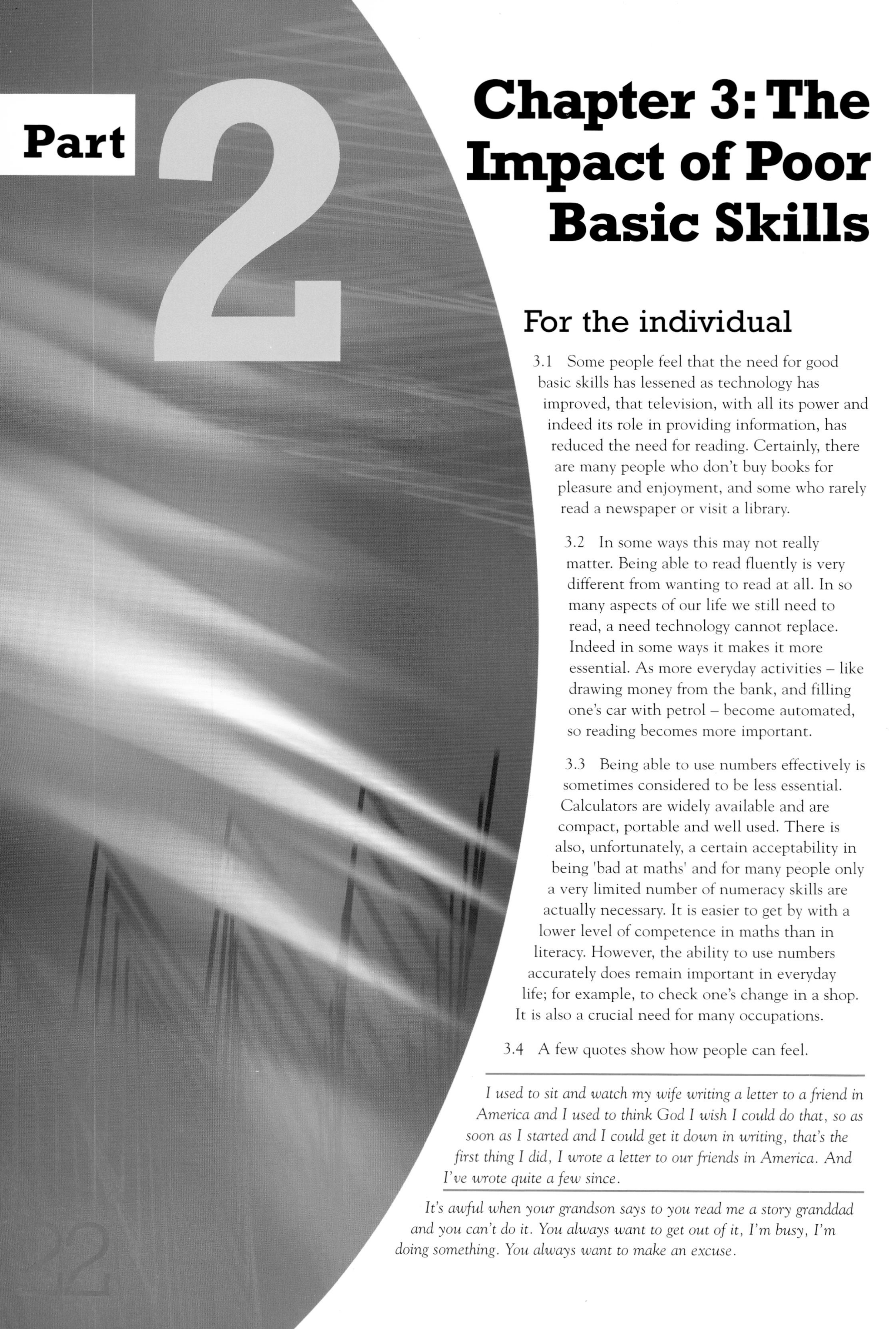

Chapter 3: The Impact of Poor Basic Skills

For the individual

3.1 Some people feel that the need for good basic skills has lessened as technology has improved, that television, with all its power and indeed its role in providing information, has reduced the need for reading. Certainly, there are many people who don't buy books for pleasure and enjoyment, and some who rarely read a newspaper or visit a library.

3.2 In some ways this may not really matter. Being able to read fluently is very different from wanting to read at all. In so many aspects of our life we still need to read, a need technology cannot replace. Indeed in some ways it makes it more essential. As more everyday activities – like drawing money from the bank, and filling one's car with petrol – become automated, so reading becomes more important.

3.3 Being able to use numbers effectively is sometimes considered to be less essential. Calculators are widely available and are compact, portable and well used. There is also, unfortunately, a certain acceptability in being 'bad at maths' and for many people only a very limited number of numeracy skills are actually necessary. It is easier to get by with a lower level of competence in maths than in literacy. However, the ability to use numbers accurately does remain important in everyday life; for example, to check one's change in a shop. It is also a crucial need for many occupations.

3.4 A few quotes show how people can feel.

I used to sit and watch my wife writing a letter to a friend in America and I used to think God I wish I could do that, so as soon as I started and I could get it down in writing, that's the first thing I did, I wrote a letter to our friends in America. And I've wrote quite a few since.

It's awful when your grandson says to you read me a story granddad and you can't do it. You always want to get out of it, I'm busy, I'm doing something. You always want to make an excuse.

It's helped me with my shopping, like all this metric and I was weighing it up to see which was cheaper, which was the best value. That was quite a challenge at first because it was remembering the metric weights etc. and I thought will it be cheaper if I buy this big one or would I be better off buying these two smaller ones. I was like testing myself all the time and am I getting conned and things like that.

I remember being on jury duty and they give us this form to fill in, well, I nearly slid under the table, I thought what am I going to do here? I got round it like, but, it was difficult.

3.5 Both literacy and numeracy have a profound effect on earnings. However, numeracy seems to have a more powerful effect than literacy. Low earnings are much more likely if one has poor basic skills than if one has good basic skills. But, as Table 3.1 shows, the difference in earnings is greater for numeracy than for literacy[11]. Similar results are found in the U.S.A[12]. Similarly, at the national level, numeracy has a profound effect on the average productivity of the workforce and explains a significant proportion of the difference in economic performance between nations[13].

3.6 A report produced for the Basic Skills Agency in 1997, *Does Numeracy Matter?*[15], is also relevant. Based on a sample of 37 year old adults who all left school at 16, it finds, for example, that whereas 30% of women with competent numeracy and low literacy earned below £150 per week, the percentage for women with very low numeracy and competent literacy was almost twice as high, at 58%.

For families

3.7 We are particularly concerned about the "intergenerational" effect of poor basic skills. Put simply, when parents have trouble with reading, writing or numeracy, it is more likely that their children will start with a similar disadvantage at school. Research by City University found that 60% of children in the lowest reading attainment group at age 10 had parents with low literacy scores; only 2% had parents with high literacy scores[16].

3.8 In short, it is likely that parents with limited basic skills will be less able to give their children a good start, or to help them if they have problems[17]. Failure to address the skills needs of adults, particularly of parents and grandparents, would therefore undermine the Government's National Literacy and Numeracy Strategies. This is one of several reasons for seeking a plan of action for adults which complements these new strategies for children.

Table 3.1 Distribution of Annual Earnings for People with Different Levels of Literacy and Numeracy[14]

Annual	Literacy		Numeracy	
earnings	Low level	High level	Low level	High level
Up to £4,600	20	11	26	6
£4,600-£9,000	29	12	29	10
£9,000-£13.000	27	16	22	17
£13.000-£19,200	17	20	15	21
Over £19,200	7	40	7	46
Total	**100**	**100**	**100**	**100**

Source: *IALS*

For communities and society

3.9 A great deal of information is available about the social characteristics of people with poor basic skills levels. These have significant consequences for the capacity of local communities to regenerate, for democratic participation, for the criminal justice system, the public health agenda and for issues of social cost and social welfare. Some key points are set out below.

Compared to those with adequate skills, adults with poor basic skills are:

- up to 5 times more likely to be unemployed or out of the labour market;
- more likely to live in a household where both partners are not in paid employment;
- more likely to have children at an earlier age, and to have more children;
- more likely to have children who also struggle with basic skills;
- less likely to own their own home;
- less likely to be in good health;
- less likely to be involved in public life, a community organisation or to vote;
- more likely to be homeless;
- over-represented in prisons and young offenders institutions.

Source:

It Doesn't Get any Better, **Bynner and Parsons, 1997**

The Basic Skills of Young Adults, **Ekynsmith and Bynner, 1994**

HM Prison Service, 1998

3.10 Of course, poor basic skills are not the sole cause of such problems. But there can be no doubt that improving an individual's basic skills can help with his or her personal and social problems, and improve the overall quality of life. This may be through making someone more employable, or more able to cope with health information and advice, or with the sort of documentation needed in arranging housing. Forms and documents are the meat and drink of welfare services – as of the rest of our bureaucratic lives – and the problems faced by people with poor reading, writing and number skills are all too obvious. Improved basic skills can help towards social inclusion and cohesion.

3.11 They can also lead to benefits for society as a whole. According to the IALS study, improved literacy can have a positive impact on the level of crime, social welfare requirements and poverty, and on improved health and community participation[18]. Although there are as yet no figures to prove it, it is a fair assumption that investments in basic skills produce savings in programmes to do with social problems, such as crime prevention.

3.12 The scale of need varies from place to place, from community to community, and, as we have said, is linked to other disadvantages and aspects of deprivation. Districts with the highest concentration of deprivation have 'roughly a quarter more adults with poor literacy or numeracy' than other areas[19]. Recent survey work for the Basic Skills Agency, using geo-demographic categories and extrapolating from 17 representative surveys, has produced a basic skills need map of England. This shows the link between deprivation and poor basic skills. However, even the area with the least need in England has a slightly higher level of need than Sweden. This shows how far we have to go.

For the economy

3.13 The employment structure of the UK has changed dramatically in recent years. The number of unskilled and semi-skilled jobs has diminished, with such jobs becoming less important to the economy. Technology, changes in working practices and sectoral changes continue to reduce the number of low skilled jobs.

3.14 Research by City University[20] underlines the significance and impact of these changes. Adults with poor basic skills are:

- most likely to end up in unskilled or semi-skilled low grade work;
- twice as likely to have been made redundant or sacked from their first job;
- four times more likely to experience long-term unemployment.

3.15 The problem might surface in a patchy career with much time spent unemployed or out of the labour market, less chance of training or promotion and in low incomes characteristic of unskilled manual jobs. With every advance up the ladder of basic skills, such problems decline. Increasingly, one will be protected against adverse labour market conditions, and helped in recovering from redundancy through re-training for new employment opportunities. Men who are out of the labour market, and have poor basic skills, not only have more difficulty getting back into jobs: they are likely to experience an actual decline in these skills.

3.16 A survey of the basic skills requirements of 1.3 million middle and lower level jobs carried out in 1993 by the Institute of Employment Studies (IES)[21], found that almost every job now requires some competence in basic skills. Furthermore, there is a considerable demand for such competence in jobs that are far from the top of the labour market. The same survey found that, if someone has not got Entry Level basic skills, 49 out of 50 jobs are closed to them, whilst 50% of jobs are closed to someone who only has Entry Level basic skills. It is also worth emphasising that, for work purposes, functional numeracy is every bit as important as functional literacy.

3.17 People at work need good basic skills not just because of the needs of a particular job. Such abilities are essential to perform a wide range of activities safely and effectively within the workplace. They have also become increasingly important because of technological changes in communication, information and production systems, the introduction of new health and safety regulations and changes in work organisation[22].

3.18 Of course, many people in jobs, but with limited basic skills, cope because of their experience and knowledge of the job. However, as jobs continue to change, and new technological, quality and work organisation systems are introduced, adults with such disadvantages may increasingly find that their lack of skills restricts their ability to adapt, and perhaps to achieve promotion.

3.19 Even if individuals often manage to cope, poor basic skills of employees can be costly to employers. This is hard to quantify. However, a survey undertaken by Gallup in 1993 estimated that basic skills problems cost the British economy more than £4.8 billion a year. This results from poor quality control, lost orders, bad communication and the need to recruit employees externally when poor skills amongst existing staff limit internal promotions. The survey suggested that on average employees with poor basic skills cost a company employing over about 50 employees £165,000 every year. This means that an average company employing 1,000 people or more could save £500 per employee if the basic skills of the workforce were improved[23]. Even this figure may be an underestimate. As Mr David Blunkett MP stated at the Literacy Task Force conference in 1997:

"Illiteracy carries economic costs as well as personal problems. The report 'Literacy, Education and Training and their Impact on the UK Economy', by Ernst and Young, suggests that illiteracy costs business and government £10 billion a year".

3.20 It is generally agreed that, if we are to achieve a world-class economy, we need a world-class workforce. To achieve this, employees and job applicants need good basic skills, not just for the current job, but for changing demands of employment. Many adults will need help to improve their skills in order to reach a level where they can not only attain employment, but are also well placed to adapt and improve their skills as the demands of the economy change. The responsibility this implies for employers is evident and critical for progress.

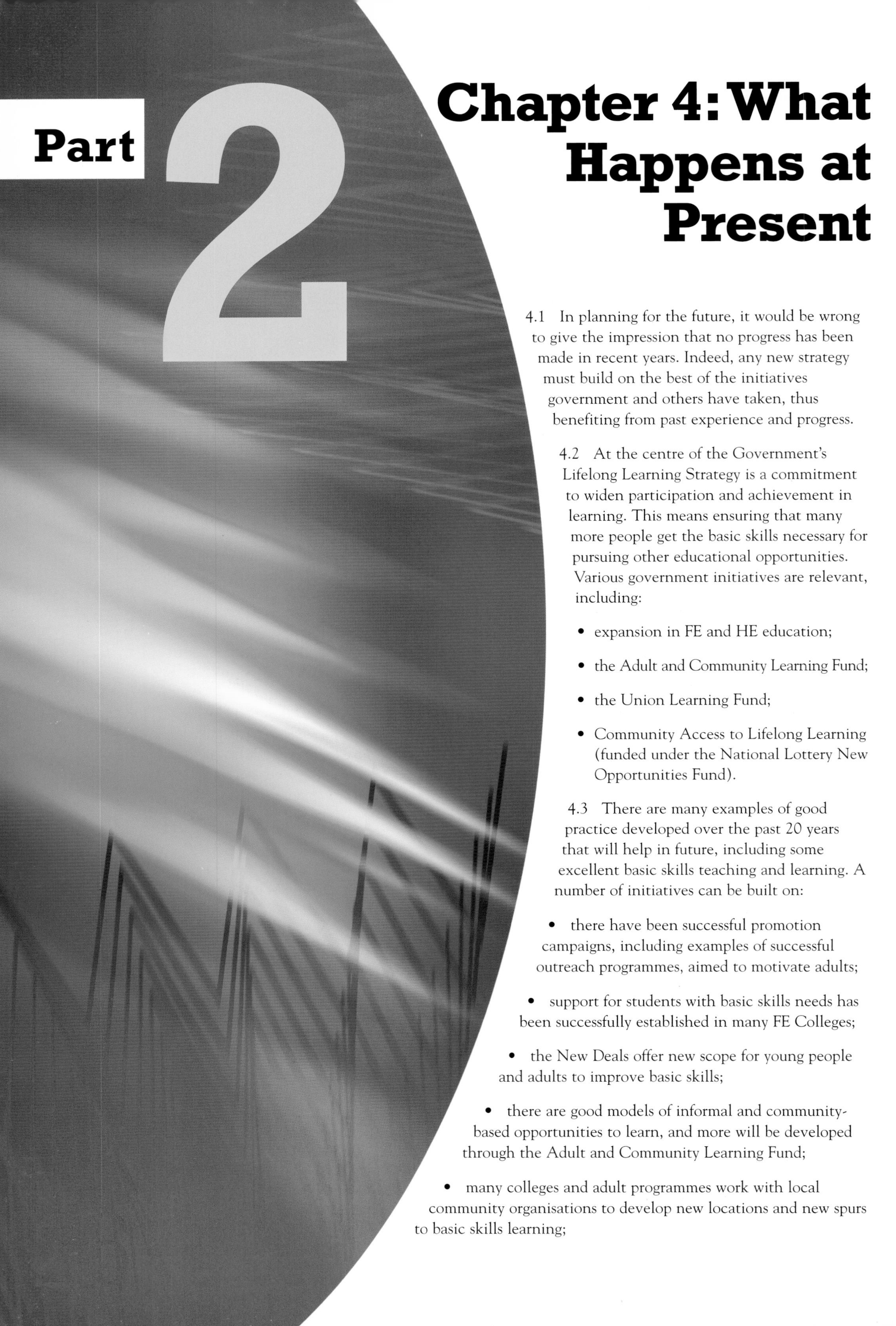

Chapter 4: What Happens at Present

4.1 In planning for the future, it would be wrong to give the impression that no progress has been made in recent years. Indeed, any new strategy must build on the best of the initiatives government and others have taken, thus benefiting from past experience and progress.

4.2 At the centre of the Government's Lifelong Learning Strategy is a commitment to widen participation and achievement in learning. This means ensuring that many more people get the basic skills necessary for pursuing other educational opportunities. Various government initiatives are relevant, including:

- expansion in FE and HE education;
- the Adult and Community Learning Fund;
- the Union Learning Fund;
- Community Access to Lifelong Learning (funded under the National Lottery New Opportunities Fund).

4.3 There are many examples of good practice developed over the past 20 years that will help in future, including some excellent basic skills teaching and learning. A number of initiatives can be built on:

- there have been successful promotion campaigns, including examples of successful outreach programmes, aimed to motivate adults;
- support for students with basic skills needs has been successfully established in many FE Colleges;
- the New Deals offer new scope for young people and adults to improve basic skills;
- there are good models of informal and community-based opportunities to learn, and more will be developed through the Adult and Community Learning Fund;
- many colleges and adult programmes work with local community organisations to develop new locations and new spurs to basic skills learning;

- family literacy programmes have drawn in large numbers of adults not previously attracted to learning and, as importantly, have forged an 'inter-generational' link between adult learning and literacy acquisition by children;
- the Basic Skills Agency Quality Mark, which lays down minimum quality standards for basic skills providers, has been achieved by over 750 programmes;
- whereas previously no qualifications for staff teaching in adult basic skills existed, some systems of initial training have now been established.

4.4 All this, together with evidence from many individuals and organisations, has convinced us that, however tough the challenge in raising standards, it can be met.

4.5 However, the scale of present provision is too limited and often patchy, due to:

- the absence of a clear national strategy;
- poor targeting of some groups of learners and lack of knowledge of the opportunities that do exist;
- a 'tip of the iceberg' scale of provision;
- inadequately trained staff;
- variable quality of programmes;
- inadequate links between quality and effectiveness of what is provided and its funding;
- incoherent inspection arrangements;
- too little diversity of opportunity;
- poor evaluation of some initiatives.

No clear national strategy

4.6 Much of the present state of affairs is due to decades with inadequate national awareness of what is at stake and without a coherent strategy. If we are to help people to improve their literacy and numeracy, what is needed above all is a clear national strategy based on targeted aims and objectives.

4.7 There are at present no clearly defined standards for what teachers should teach and what learners should learn. In practice this means that there is no core curriculum for teaching basic skills, no clear national quality standards, and no clear idea of what learners should be aiming to achieve.

4.8 The Prison Education Service however, is a good example of how an effective strategy can work. The Service has taken action to improve the quality of provision by:

- requiring that all providers hold the Basic Skills Agency Quality Mark;
- introducing a new core curriculum;
- ensuring that all prisons have plans to assess how prisoners with basic skills needs will be supported in the workplace;
- providing training to civilian instructors and prison officers to support these needs;
- setting challenging targets for improvement in basic skills.

Poor targeting and lack of knowledge of the opportunities that exist

4.9 Although adults with basic skills problems are not a single homogenous group, all too often they have been treated in this way. Targeting has been crude, and in trying to encourage participation, too little effort has been made to identify the nature of the group concerned. Perhaps as a result, some groups are under-represented, particularly those with the most severe difficulties.

4.10 At present, the vast majority of people with literacy and numeracy problems are not in programmes. Some of this is due to lack of knowledge of what might be at stake, and how much they might gain from improvement. This is borne out in the testimonies from people who ultimately did join programmes.

4.11 For many others, doing something about basic skills is not a priority. There is a widespread culture of low expectations, a memory of unhappy school years, leading to little enthusiasm for "going back into the classroom", not to mention the stigma associated with admitting basic inabilities. Changing this complex culture will not be easy, but must be the aim.

4.12 Equally, knowledge of where good – or any – programmes are available is often too hard to come by. Research by City University suggested that many people with the problems we are discussing did not know that help was available.[24]

'Tip of the iceberg' scale of provision

4.13 At the moment, what is happening is too small-scale. We have been struck, indeed shocked, by the patchiness – almost a random patchiness – of what is available. Whether provision exists in an area depends too much on whether a major education provider, such as a college, TEC or an LEA adult education service, thinks it important. Often this comes down to whether the head of the institution is keen. In one area there might be extensive, well-resourced, provision with thousands of learners, whilst in a neighbouring area there might be little or no provision. And even where provision does exist, it is often regarded as marginal, a "Cinderella" service. What exists is too often on the margins of other education and training provision. Overall, there just isn't enough available provision.This cannot continue.

4.14 The situation is illustrated by the availability of basic skills support in FE Colleges. The fact is that as many as 1 in 3 students in such colleges has poor literacy and as many as 50% poor numeracy, which may cause them problems in their general course work. This may explain why – according to a survey undertaken by the Audit Commission and HMI in 1993 – typically between 30% and 40% of students starting on a course do not achieve the qualifications they set out for. Providing support for basic skills in colleges undoubtedly improves this situation, increasing retention and achievement and reducing drop-out. The Basic Skills Agency found in 1997 that 3 in 4 students who needed and received support completed their courses or first year successfully, compared with only half of those who needed support but did not get it.[25] Yet many students in colleges – varying considerably from college to college – who require support with basic skills are never offered it.[26]

4.15 This randomness of provision also affects programmes for the unemployed. The New Deals have provided the best opportunity in years for unemployed adults who need help to improve their basic skills. However, the extent to which adults are able to get support differs greatly, depending on how aware different Employment Service Personal Advisors are of these particular needs, and on the priority they give to them.

Not all staff are properly trained

4.16 The quality of teaching is crucial. We are aware of the many skilled and dedicated teachers working in this area, but specific training for teachers is nowhere near universal. This cannot continue. For example, the FEFC's recent report on Programme Area 10 states that:

"Unlike staff in other programme areas, basic education staff frequently have no relevant qualification for the area in which they teach. Some teachers lack general teaching qualifications and others lack specialist qualifications, for example, qualifications in teaching basic skills and ESOL".

4.17 Though the take-up of initial training, particularly among volunteers, has been high, the development of higher level skills is uncoordinated. For example, the main in-service qualification for basic skills teachers is the City & Guilds Certificate in Teaching Basic Skills 9285. There is however little consistency of approach in the delivery of training for the certificate, and take-up is poor. While some 200 centres are now registered to deliver the award, and over 13,000 part-time and full-time paid teachers are involved in basic skills programmes nationally, only about 2,000 staff have this more demanding qualification.

4.18 Much of the reason for the current lack of training is the balance of full-time and part-time teachers. Less than 1 in 10 is full-time and more than 1 in 3 are employed for less than 6 hours a week. This necessarily restricts the amount of continuous professional training that teachers are able or willing to go for.

4.19 The fact that basic skills teaching remains an area where there are few career opportunities or opportunities for professional development means that it still largely remains an unattractive career path. This is not to say that people don't want to teach basic skills. But it does make it more difficult to recruit new teachers.

4.20 In essence the best-trained teachers in our education system are teaching enthusiastic young children at Key Stage 1. Those with least opportunities for professional development, and with most job insecurity, are teaching adults who have often failed at school and need intensive help.

Quality of provision is variable and there is a poor link between quality and funding

4.21 There is at present too little incentive for the least good providers to improve what they do. In short, there is too weak a link between the quality and effectiveness of what is provided and its funding. A college, adult education service or training provider, which makes available high quality and effective basic skills teaching for adults, gets funded in the same way as a neighbouring equivalent, content with poor quality and ineffective provision.

4.22 Many individuals and organisations have complained that project-based regeneration funding for basic skills sometimes constrains essential outreach work, and encourages over-simple outputs. There is said to be a 'bidding culture', with progress depending on competitive bidding for small sums to be spent over a short period. We share the concern that time and energy can be wasted in bidding for short-term funding from several different organisations with different funding criteria. Such confusion is discouraging.

4.23 The existing FEFC funding mechanism also has weaknesses. For example it can fail to take account of the way a college serving a widespread and partly rural area needs to operate if it is to meet the needs of its diverse community. Some programmes inevitably cost more than others, not because they are inefficient, but because outreach and out-centre provision is more costly. The present funding mechanism requires change.

4.24 Opportunities to achieve a guaranteed baseline of quality in programmes have not always been taken on by funders. The Basic Skills Agency Quality Mark sets out minimum quality standards for basic skills programmes, and is now held by more than 750 basic skills programmes for adults in England. However, the award is voluntary and funding does not relate to it. The exception is in prison basic skills programmes, where all providers must hold the Quality Mark.

4.25 The FEFC has recognised that some basic skills courses suffer from insufficient arrangements for Quality Assurance. For example, when weaknesses are identified through inspection, institutions seldom produce action plans for improvement[27]. The FEFC's new Quality Initiative is likely to lead to improvement in Quality Assurance mechanisms, but more must be done to guarantee high quality all round.

Inspection arrangements lack coherence

4.26 Chances for a common national quality framework are weakened by the involvement of three separate Inspection Agencies (FEFC, OFSTED and the Training Standards Council (TSC)) each using different approaches. Though some joint work has been undertaken to harmonise methods and, though all Inspectorates see the need for a common approach, this has not yet been achieved.

4.27 Part of the weakness also stems from the existing inspection grading system, which can be subject to anomalies. For example, the Training Standards Council, which is responsible for the inspection of training programmes for unemployed adults, has stated its concern that, on the 5-point scale used by the three inspection organisations, all the organisations inspected by the TSC had been assessed at Grade 3 or better. Yet the overall conclusion was that there were serious weaknesses in:

'screening and initial assessment; some poor quality training sessions; inappropriately qualified staff; poor links between basic skills provision and vocational programmes; insufficient and inappropriate learning materials and learning is assessment driven'.

Evidence from the Training Standards Council

Not enough coherence in diversity of opportunity

4.28 We were struck by the limited choice of provision available to adults who wish to improve their basic skills. This applies both to the type and the intensity of existing programmes. In terms of intensity, nearly all learners are in part-time programmes, and 70% attend for between 2-4 hours per week (an average of 90 hours per year).

4.29 The limited amount of direct teaching time available on most courses means that progress for learners is inevitably slow. Of course, some of them do not want to attend for more than a few hours a week, and others are prohibited from doing more by pressures of time and responsibility. This is a serious limitation. Evidence both from this country and the USA shows that such limited teaching means that a learner would need many years to get to the 'threshold' basic skills level. In the USA, the research shows that between 550-600 hours of instruction are needed to become fully literate and numerate.[28] At the rate we provide currently, it would take many years for most learners to achieve such progress.

4.30 Also, despite the development of pilot programmes in new areas, and evidence from the Basic Skills Agency[29] of effective styles of provision, diversity in the type of provision available is still limited.

4.31 FE Colleges and literacy and numeracy courses account for the greatest percentage of learners, but development of other routes for provision is quite slow. As a result, present provision is not sufficiently varied to respond to the varying motivations and needs of adults. We are particularly concerned about the inadequate scale of community and workplace provision.

4.32 Community-based programmes can reach out to individuals and groups not attracted to more traditional programmes. They can avoid the stigma associated with formal educational institutions. However, only a small proportion of basic skills learners are able to access community-based provision. This is largely due to the lack of a specific funding source. The formal funding system, with its emphasis on colleges, has not been flexible enough to allow community organisations and groups to get involved in a way that suits their clients. Often they have had to fall back on short-term funding, such as the Single Regeneration Budget, the European Social Fund or Charitable Trusts, which help an organisation to get started, but have rarely led to sustainable development.

4.33 It is surprising, indeed discouraging, to find that few employers are involved in basic skills work and that, on the whole, there is so little provision at the workplace. This is surprising given the well-researched link between good basic skills, employability and company performance. The latest Skills Needs in Britain survey suggests that 1 in 5 employers are now providing training opportunities, some of which hopefully cover basic skills. But few offer the quantity or quality of support necessary to lead to significant improvements in individual skills levels or in the ability of employees to improve their job effectiveness. Well-known schemes exist, mostly in large companies like Ford and Nissan. However, thus far, even in large companies and even where there are other training involvements, basic skills receive a sadly low priority.

4.34 The Basic Skills at Work project increased basic skills training in the workplace and made TECs more aware of basic skills needs. Unfortunately, in spite of positive results, funding was not available to continue the programme, and to replicate the successful models elsewhere. The continuation of programmes was left to the commitment of individual TECs, colleges and companies and although some institutions have developed sustainable programmes, such as the excellent programme at Telford College of Arts and Technology, further development has been stunted by lack of funding and support in companies and educational institutions.

4.35 This has also happened in the United States and Canada. In both, continued provision of basic skills programmes has depended on Federal, State or Provincial support. In general, when that support diminished, so did the number and scope of workplace programmes.

Initiatives have not been evaluated effectively enough

4.36 There have been various short-term initiatives and measures. But often in the past, good initiatives have not been built on, and sometimes have even been abandoned. So, whilst successful work was being undertaken to develop workplace programmes with employers, for example, Workbase, the Basic Skills at Work initiative and the work of the Industrial Language Training Unit, none resulted in long-term action. There are other examples of how community groups and voluntary organisations can help those with literacy and numeracy needs, but again many projects have not been turned into long-term, sustainable action.

4.37 The current context for basic skills is positive. The Government has introduced a number of initiatives aimed at motivating new learners, widening participation, and providing more opportunities for those with poor basic skills to improve their lot. The commitment to tackle social exclusion is also helpful.

4.38 In sum, it is clear that much good practice does exist, for example in support for students in colleges, and in the work of providers and community groups. However, the scale of the problem is so great that this alone is not enough. Adults with poor basic skills remain largely unmotivated, the choice of provision is too limited to meet the needs of learners, and the availability and quality of provision is too variable. More must be done. The remainder of our report will suggest the way forward.

Chapter 5: A National Strategy and National Targets

5.1 Our broad vision is clear, aiming at a transformation for the millions of adults with basic skills problems. We have described the present state of play, showing how challenging that transformation needs to be. To set the scene for the future, we bring together the essence of our strategic approach, which we think of as a truly Fresh Start.

- The problem the country faces is substantial and urgent: not to tackle it as a national priority is not an acceptable option;
- it is on a larger scale than in most advanced countries;
- it has a serious impact on individuals and families, and indeed on the economy and the state of society as a whole;
- it has a serious effect on opportunities for a full life for the 1 in 5 adults with poor literacy and the 1 in 5 with very poor numeracy;
- present provision is unacceptably variable and limited in scale and choice;
- provision is of variable quality and incoherent, with availability determined too much by chance;
- for a range of reasons, many connected with the above deficiencies, only some 250,000 of the 7 or so million adults with poor basic skills are currently in study programmes.

5.2 The National Strategy we propose aims to deal with this. Although it will take time to work through to every area of England, it could have an initial impact very quickly. That must be the aim. It requires better planning, an emphasis on local partnerships, clearer criteria for funding, better quality and more diverse learning opportunities, and improved and sustained promotion and recruitment. A combination of these advances will achieve a dramatic rise in participation.

5.3 The strategy aims to create a context in which adults with poor basic skills:

- are able to choose from a diverse range of accessible study opportunities, selecting those which best fit their individual needs, responsibilities and life styles;
- are entitled to free, confidential and high quality assessment, advice and guidance;
- are assured that any programme they join will be of high quality and will help them to gain the skills necessary to participate and progress in society, employment, and a full family and personal life;
- can choose, in deciding between routes towards a qualification, between coursework-based assessments and tests, including a new national test;
- are motivated to improve their skills because of all of the above and because they are aware of the benefits that follow.

5.4 Our proposals for the National Strategy are based on certain key principles, namely that the Strategy will:

- focus above all on the needs, aspirations, motivation and achievements of individual learners; and with this in mind should clearly set out what potential learners are entitled to in terms of baseline assessment, information, guidance, programmes of study, assessment and qualifications;
- embrace the determination and achievement of clear national targets, not only for the number of learners it is hoped will participate in programmes, but also for standards in provision; hence it should:
    - include a National Framework of Standards and Qualifications in basic skills, covering curricula, teaching standards, methods of assessment, inspection methods and qualifications as such;
    - incorporate moves towards funding arrangements which are affordable, and which are only available for programmes that meet adequate standards;
    - ensure that teaching arrangements throughout the country and in all sectors, including industry, business and community contexts, are readily accessible and attractive to potential learners;
    - ultimately be the responsibility of the Department for Education and Employment, but involve other relevant government departments and other principal partners at national level (i.e. the Qualifications and Curriculum Authority (QCA), the Basic Skills Agency (BSA), the Further Education Funding Council (FEFC) and the University for Industry (UfI)), as well as local partners in Lifelong Learning Partnerships, such as Further Education Colleges, local authorities, the Careers Service and Training and Enterprise Councils, employers, trade unions and voluntary organisations;
    - ensure national awareness and commitment through continuous promotional and marketing campaigns;
    - ensure, equally, that adequate research, data collection and monitoring arrangements support its implementation.

5.5 The ultimate target should be the virtual elimination of poor basic skills. This is highly ambitious, but must be the long-term aim if we want to rid society of the frustration and waste that these problems bring. But the strategy must have clear milestones towards this long-term aim, these targets should be strictly monitored over time.

5.6 We have been impressed by the effectiveness of the new national targets for literacy and numeracy at Key Stage 2 in schools in motivating and generating concerted action. Supported by LEA and school targets, they have provided a clear focus for raising standards in primary schools and are the centrepiece of the National Literacy and National Numeracy Strategies. A similar approach is required for adults.

5.7 Indeed it is essential that the National Strategy be developed so as to complement the existing strategies for schools.

5.8 There is already, in *The Learning Age*, a national target for increasing participation by adults in basic skills programmes to 500,000 per annum by 2002. As part of this, the University for Industry (UfI) has a target to provide support for 200,000 adults with basic skills needs over three years. These are important targets. Ultimately, however, there should be a more ambitious target for improving the basic skills of the approximately 20% of adults with poor literacy, and the 40% or more of adults with poor numeracy. The targets must be set urgently and deliberately so that the long and medium-term improvement is set in train. As we have said, the final aim must be virtually to eliminate poor basic skills. But, such are the many years of under-performance behind us, and the scale of the problem, that this can only be very long-term. We do not therefore propose a target date for this ultimate achievement, focusing rather on the milestones towards the challenging targets for 2010.

5.9 In setting targets, one must take into account the current state of play, the hurdles in the way, and the inevitable pressure on resources. Taking all these into account, we propose that by 2010 the aim should be to reduce by half the number of adults of working age with low literacy. This would raise the level of functional literacy in England from 80% to 90%, and means lifting some 3.5 million adults out of low literacy over this period. It is also at least as important to reduce the level of low numeracy and we therefore propose a second objective of reducing the number of adults with low numeracy by the same number i.e by 3.5 million adults by the year 2010. This would raise the number of numerate adults from around 60% to 70%: a higher aim, however desirable in principle, would be unrealistic, given where we are starting from and the enormous difficulties in the way. A higher target can be achieved – as we suggest below – for those with "very low" numeracy.

5.10 It is always in our minds that, once an adult has achieved functional literacy or numeracy, he or she should have every encouragement and opportunity to achieve basic or key skill qualifications at Level 2 and beyond. We support the intention of the Government to devise a national target for key skills as soon as robust measures have been developed.

5.11 To get 9 out of 10 people to a level where they can undertake Level 1 literacy tasks effectively, and to enable 2 out of 3 adults to complete simple numeracy tasks, may seem modest targets. However, ambition needs to be balanced with realism. We have years of under-education to cope with, when standards failed to keep pace with changing requirements and demands, with low expectation becoming all too ingrained. If these targets can be achieved by 2010, England will be close to where Sweden is today on literacy.

5.12 In deciding on the targets, it is vital to take account of:

- the small minority of people who may not be able to improve their basic skills to Level 1 because of serious learning difficulties[30];
- likely levels of immigration into the UK in the coming years, and the vital group of people for whom English is not the first language.

5.13 One must also take into account the reduction in the number of school-leavers needing further help as a result of the National Literacy and National Numeracy Strategies. These will eventually reduce the flow of adults with problems.

5.14 It is also sensible to remember that, amongst those with poor literacy and/or numeracy, there will inevitably be quite a number who, however accessible and good the teaching programmes, may have no desire to improve. This is why we have in mind the virtual elimination of functional illiteracy and innumeracy, rather than a 100% target.

5.15 Table 5.1 sets out our proposed literacy and numeracy targets for all adults and also specifically for young people. These are inevitably orders of magnitude, and clearly the long-term targets will ultimately depend on what has been achieved by the year 2002 (already Government policy) and by our target year 2005.

5.16 We believe that the proposals in this report will result in achieving the overall target of 500,000 participants by 2002 set in our terms of reference. Beyond that the targets we propose should be refined, with the help of a Government baseline survey, to include year-on-year progress towards the intermediate years and the 2010 targets. Success will depend on the changes we now turn to in the following chapters, and ultimately on the resources dedicated to the task.

Table 5.1: Possible targets for 2005 and 2010 (percentages)*

	Now	2005	2010
Literacy			
All adults	80	84	90
People aged 19	83	90	95
Numeracy			
All adults	60	64	70
People aged 19	60	85	90

RECOMMENDATION 1 – A National Basic Skills Strategy for Adults

The Government should launch a National Strategy to reduce the number of adults with low levels of basic skills.

RECOMMENDATION 2 – Targets

(i) As part of the National Strategy, the Government should commit itself to the virtual elimination of functional illiteracy and innumeracy.

(ii) In addition to the accepted participation target for 2002, the Government should set specific basic skills targets for adults and for young people to be achieved by 2005 and 2010, on the scale proposed in the new National Strategy.

**1 The figures in the Now column are our best broad estimates, taking into account the IALS survey and the work of the Centre for Longitudinal Studies at the Institute of Education (see Annex A).*

2 As we have explained in the text, the Numeracy figures are problematical and so inevitably are the targets. We have here given figures for numeracy as a whole (including "low" and "very low" numeracy). Two points need to be made.

a) the big jump for people aged 19, between now and the 2005 target, reflects other Government initiatives which will help in reaching and motivating greater numbers of young people;

b)as a comparison, if we were to estimate figures for "very low" numeracy only, this would suggest (for all adults) moving from 80% to 90% in 2010; and (for people aged 19) from 80% now to 95% in 2010.

Chapter 6: Increasing Participation

6.1 One of our key aims is to find ways of making the overall arrangements so attractive that far more people will positively want to take advantage of them. This means, not least, that if one has a real problem with reading, writing, language or numbers, one should be aware of it, should see it as a problem and be conscious of the benefits that could come from making progress. The stigma felt by many who have serious problems has to be totally understood in the arrangements on offer.

6.2 To address these issues, national awareness of the extent of basic skills problems will have to be raised, and the impact they can have on individual lives. The benefits that can come from having good basic skills must be more clearly shown. The role of the national and local media are central to these tasks, given their ability to reach and influence large numbers of people. In addition, there must be increased local and community activity, including outreach work and more use of both statutory and community agencies as referral points.

6.3 Once interested, adults must be given easy access to helpful information, advice and guidance. Time and again research has shown that people are not aware that help is available; that there may be study possibilities available in their area, some of which may fit their needs. We know that most adults who drop out of basic skills courses do so in the first few weeks, usually because the course doesn't suit their needs, or is not what they expected[31]. So, high quality guidance is essential to ensure that more adults get help to find the right study possibilities.

The media

6.4 The broadcast media, particularly the BBC, have played a crucial role in promoting basic skills and keeping the issue before the public. From the initial 'On the Move' campaign in the mid-1970s, the BBC has continued with its effective commitment to improving the basic skills of adults through campaigns such as *Spelling it Out* and *Read and Write Together*.

The first UK Adult Literacy campaign which ran from 1975 to 1978, is still regarded as being one of the best examples of what a "massive contribution to recruitment of learners and volunteer tutors and to public awareness can be made by broadcasting"[32]. This involved entertaining prime time television and radio programmes. Over the three years of the campaign, 125,000 learners had been helped to improve their reading and writing, and 75,000 volunteers had been trained.

6.5 In Independent Television, there have also been good contributions. For example, in the 1980s, Yorkshire Television led the way in programmes in basic numeracy. As part of the Year of Reading, Channel 4 has linked literacy promotion to their popular *Brookside*. The community units of the ITV companies have for many years contributed to promotional basic skills campaigns.

6.6 The BSA's regional promotion campaigns, using local TV and radio advertising to encourage people with poor basic skills to call the Agency's 0800 National Referral Service telephone number, have increased referrals[33]. 75% of callers said that, though they had been thinking about improving their skills, the TV and radio adverts encouraged them to call.

6.7 There is evidence that the *targeting* of promotion, focusing on specific needs or concerns, can be very effective. For example, the growing sophistication of broadcast-led campaigns, and their ability to target specific groups, is illustrated by the experience of the *Read and Write Together* campaign[34]. This was developed in 1995 by the BBC in partnership with the Basic Skills Agency. These 'advertisements' targeted parents with poor basic skills and emphasised how much this could cause problems for their childrens' literacy development. Over 300,000 people responded to the campaign over a four-week period – the largest response to any similar social action campaign to date. Sophisticated marketing techniques had been used in the design of the promotional 'shorts', and they were placed at peak times on BBC TV when the target audience were known to be watching.[35]

6.8 In short, there is considerable evidence that the media are effective in motivating adults to join basic skills programmes. We were therefore encouraged by our talks with broadcasters and their keenness to help further in this area. But we are not thinking of a one-off high-profile campaign. This would have, at best, a short-term impact and may even give the wrong impression that there isn't a long-standing problem. If our long-term ambitions are to be realised, broadcasters – TV and radio – should be mobilised for a continuing crusade. To create interest and encouragement does indeed require a "big bang" campaign for launching the Fresh Start, but to maintain momentum and progress thereafter, the media should be encouraged to plan continuing campaigns.

6.9 "Market segmentation" of such campaigns will be more effective than attempting a catch-all approach. We need to attract adults at key stages of their domestic and working lives, with campaigns that link to their current needs and aspirations, and which offer a solution through improving their basic skills. Promotion campaigns need to excite potential learners in the context of:

- work;
- helping their children;
- getting a particular qualification;
- dealing with everyday life;
- being more involved in the community.

6.10 Broadcasters agree that raising the awareness of adults with poor basic skills requires approaches which go well beyond the educational context. Subtle ways of incorporating literacy and numeracy issues in popular programmes (lifestyle programmes, quiz shows, etc.) are a necessary and promising route.

6.11 One of the most powerful needs for literacy remains the ability to read a newspaper. Mass circulation newspapers, with their flair for simplifying key issues, are therefore well placed to join in the proposed crusade. They should do so, not only because it is in their interests, but because it is a clear responsibility to make adults aware of the issues and – hopefully – of the attractive offerings on hand.

6.12 We also had in mind the potential usefulness of broader promotional initiatives and campaigns, including the Campaign for Learning and Learning Direct.

6.13 The University for Industry (UfI) will be a key actor in promoting relevant programmes. Its task is to develop the demand for lifelong learning. It will market its new learning opportunities, which, given their flexibility, should in themselves increase demand and motivation. The UfI will look for new ways to reach adults and to motivate them to improve their basic skills. In some cases this will require the creative thinking available in the media and advertising worlds. It is also an area where much can be learned from abroad. For instance, ABC Canada[36] receives more than $4 million of advertising support for their public awareness campaigns each year. A similar approach to corporate sponsorship might work here.

6.14 We therefore recommend that a promotion group comprising UfI, broadcast media and press representatives, advertising and marketing agencies, the Basic Skills Agency and others should be given the task of identifying the most effective ways to promote basic skills, and the clearest routes for adults to get into programmes. This should be done with a view to launching a continuous high-profile campaign in 2000.

6.15 At present, broadcasters see their primary role as one of promotion and of raising the attention of the public. However, the development of digital technology means that a direct teaching role may soon become more accessible. Channel 4 and the Basic Skills Agency are involved in a project aimed to develop basic skills learning programmes for the UfI that can be delivered through digital television, going all the way from assessment to accreditation. We hope that the UfI will continue to keep a focus on provision that can be delivered directly into people's homes. This is a way of helping both with motivation and access.

Referral by local and community agencies

6.16 Many intermediary organisations and individuals are already in contact with adults with poor basic skills. Their involvement needs to be harnessed to contribute to the success of the National Strategy. They must be given the necessary information and motivation to act as initial signposts to teaching opportunities. This can include Citizens Advice Bureaux, the probation service, Job Centres, the Benefits Agency, tenants associations, drug rehabilitation centres, employers, librarians, health visitors and so on. Given the many social characteristics correlated with poor basic skills, a cross-sector approach to information and guidance is crucial.

6.17 Local agencies are often well placed to identify basic skills problems in wider contexts. Advice workers in the Citizens Advice Bureaux come across countless examples of adults needing help because they can't understand a letter received from the Council, or are having trouble with their budgeting because of problems with numbers. A health visitor is in an ideal position to identify a mother or father having trouble with printed health information relating to their child.

6.18 Of course, many organisations running basic skills programmes already encourage the referral of potential learners from local statutory agencies and community groups. However, many others lack the information to carry out this role effectively. There is evidence that potential learners referred by third party agencies and organisations drop-out of programmes more frequently than others[37]. Equally, there is evidence that drop-outs can be reduced if such third party agencies and organisations appreciate better what programmes are available locally, how these programmes work, and what commitment and effort is required.

6.19 The Government has set out its aim to improve the quality and coverage of local Information, Advice and Guidance (IAG) services. This will be achieved by:

- investing substantial additional resources in the development of IAG services at a local level;
- contracting with partnerships of local providers for the delivery of these services in each area of the country; and
- requiring all providers in receipt of public funds to comply with appropriate quality standards from 2001.

6.20 Some of the resources allocated to developing IAG services locally should be used to link statutory and community agencies into the IAG network. The aim should be to create a team of front-line advice and guidance workers from staff already working in agencies such as the Employment Service, Citizens Advice Bureau, Probation Service and tenants groups. We have been impressed by the example of Union Learning Representatives, para-professionals who are able to:

- provide accurate information;
- provide initial advice;
- signpost to other sources of advice and guidance.

6.21 We propose that the new Lifelong Learning Partnerships – discussed in a later chapter – should take responsibility for developing this expanded network of specialist and front-line IAG workers. This will involve:

- short initial training courses in advice and guidance for existing staff in key agencies;
- the production and dissemination of materials for key statutory and community organisations mapping out what opportunities are available for adults with poor basic skills in the local area, and progression routes between these programmes.

Outreach

6.22 To reach adults who have little contact with statutory or even community agencies requires increased emphasis on outreach work. This can build on much good practice already in existence. For example, an action research project examining the effectiveness of different types of recruitment, found that the approach of a door-to-door salesman was the biggest source of recruitment. As one provider commented:

"this followed the experience of other organisations taking a service to, or selling to, the lowest socio-economic groups. Historically, family insurance and membership of the Labour Party were expanded in the same way – particularly among people with few educational opportunities. The fact that the results and improvements claimed for any of these services and products are long term, abstract and sometimes complicated, has not proved a barrier to expansion. It would seem therefore that similarly an educational service needs to be 'sold' at a personal level if those most in need are to participate".

RECOMMENDATION 3 – National Promotion Campaign

There should be a continuous high profile promotion campaign, with clear segmentation for different target groups of learners, to be devised by a new Adult Basic Skills Promotion Task Force. This should be set up in 2000.

Chapter 7: Entitlement

7.1 It is crucial for learners to have a clear entitlement to high quality:

- initial assessment;
- professional advice and guidance;
- wide choice of learning opportunity;
- effective teaching.

Initial assessment

7.2 Individuals without a recognised qualification in English or maths – and everyone for whom English is not their first language – should be entitled to a free confidential assessment of basic skills, whether employed or unemployed. They should be able to get an assessment without enrolling on a programme, and free assessment could be available through a short assessment test in libraries, job centres, community centres and on-line. At the least, it will tell individuals whether they need to improve their literacy or numeracy and, if so, where they might get guidance.

Advice and guidance

7.3 Guidance and information on basic skills courses need to be freely available to all potential learners. Toll free call lines, such as that operated by the Basic Skills Agency and Learning Direct, will be a powerful tool. The University for Industry will be a vital new source of information. In addition, major publicity should be undertaken – through broadcasters and the press – to publicise arrangements for free assessment, advice and guidance.

Release from work

7.4 Making more intensive teaching available will be of little use unless people who are interested have the time to pursue it. Hence we wish to see day release arrangements improved: we enlarge on this point in the next chapter.

Choice

7.5 Adults with poor basic skills should have a wide choice of provision. They are not a homogenous group. They have diverse needs and motivations, different levels of skill and differing pressures in their lives. They will not all want to learn in a particular way and at a particular place. Some will prefer to join a programme at a college, some would only respond to an opportunity if it is at their place of work. Others still would be keener if there are opportunities in a library, local community centre, arts centre and so forth. Programmes incorporated in other activities – health, housing, arts, sport etc. – may be the most appealing of all.

7.6 Participation by learners clearly increases when a variety of opportunities are available to suit their needs, preferences and lifestyles. A good example is the experience of Cornwall LEA's basic skills provision, *Link into Learning*. This increased the number of adults taking part by almost 10%, by providing a greater range of more flexible learning opportunities and by focusing courses on specific needs and sectors[38]. Successful recruitment has as much to do with availability and diversity of opportunities as with promotional campaigns.

7.7 Programmes should be easy to get to, in busy well-populated areas, served by good public transport, well sign-posted and safe at night. In rural areas, transport difficulties and travel costs are sometimes a barrier, and imaginative approaches are required to overcome such hurdles. But some programmes have been successful even in such difficult conditions and there is much good experience to build on. For example, Somerset LEA developed an effective network of small basic skills open learning centres in different areas of the county. Part of the attraction was supported self-study, including 'distance learning', with learners going to the centre mainly to collect assignments or to attend assessment sessions. But, when short-term central funding ended, these centres were gradually closed.

7.8 In short, what is needed is a wider range of learning opportunities in every area. These must cover:

- programmes for young people;
- programmes for the unemployed;
- workplace programmes;
- basic skills support programmes;
- community based programmes, including programmes that link improvement of basic skills to economic and social regeneration of communities;
- specific literacy and numeracy courses;
- family programmes, such as family literacy and family numeracy.

7.9 Of course, not everyone can take up every opportunity. Some opportunities are only available to people who are unemployed, or at work or enrolled as students on a college course.

7.10 Although choice is crucial, it must not mean diverse standards of quality or a lack of coherence. Indeed, in the proposed National Strategy, coherence and achievement of high standards is crucial.

Effective teaching

7.11 The targets will only be reached if people who want to improve their basic skills find themselves entitled to the necessary teaching, free of charge. This is a matter of elementary justice. People can get free full-time education up to 19 and, if they qualify, higher education, all subsidised. It is only fair that those who missed out early in life should have the right to free help in acquiring basic skills.

7.12 All learners must be entitled to high quality and effective teaching. How they are taught, what they are taught, how they are assessed and what they achieve, all these key aspects are part and parcel of clear national quality standards. It is particularly important, in view of the proven effectiveness of Information and Communication Technology (ICT), that learners should be entitled to ready access to relevant technology, including hardware and software. We return to this point in Chapter 9.

7.13 Research submitted to us suggests that, ideally, adults should get substantial periods of intensive tuition, to enable them to move quickly and effectively towards command of basic skills. The predominant 2-4 hours a week during conventional academic terms implies such a slow rate of progress that many learners drop-out in frustration. The limitations of very limited teaching are best expressed in a report from the USA[39], which describes learners as enrolling in programmes functionally illiterate, making progress, but still leaving functionally illiterate. A similar situation must occur here with too many learners not reaching the threshold of functionality.

7.14 We considered specifying an entitlement to a specific number of hours of teaching over a given period. On balance, however, we do not think this has much merit. For one thing, it would imply that one can determine accurately the numbers of hours needed to reach a particular level, given that learners begin from such different starting points. For another, it suggests that, when the number of hours of teaching has been used up, the entitlement ends. This would give the wrong message, particularly to those with the most serious difficulties.

7.15 More intensive courses and opportunities need to be made available at different times of the week and at different times of the year. A recent survey suggested that many potential learners would favour courses at the weekend[40], yet few such courses exist. The success of the recent Summer Schools run by colleges also shows the demand for flexibility.

Individual Learning Accounts

7.16 We examined the role that might be played by the new Individual Learning Accounts (ILAs) in encouraging adults to join basic skills programmes and to complete their courses. Clearly, if ILAs are to make a difference, they must be taken up by those who are not already active participants in learning.

7.17 The Government has stated its commitment to make basic skills learning opportunities available free of charge, which means that ILAs do not have a direct role to play in basic skills provision. What we propose is a dynamic use of Individual Learning Accounts for basic skills learners which will encourage adults to build on the skills they have acquired, and become 'lifelong learners'.

7.18 We recommend that adults who have successfully completed basic skills courses should be a priority target for the first million Individual Learning Accounts funded from TEC resources. Such an initiative would reward individual commitment to learning, and open the doors to further progress and wider participation.

RECOMMENDATION 4 – Entitlement

(i) All adults with basic skills below Level 2 should be entitled to a confidential assessment of their skills on demand, access to free, high quality information advice and guidance, and access to a variety of programmes of study – all free of charge.

(ii) People who have successfully completed basic skills courses should be a priority target for the first million Individual Learning Accounts funded from TEC resources to help them progress.

(iii) The Government should consider how, in the long term, Individual Learning Accounts can be most effectively used to motivate these learners.

Chapter 8: Expanding & Improving Opportunities

8.1 There has to be a rapid expansion in the scale and diversity of opportunities available to help adults to improve their basic skills. Current provision meets little more than the 'tip of the iceberg' of need, and unless more and more effective opportunities exist the needed transformation in national life will not be achieved.

8.2 However, whilst expanding the scale of what is available, consistency and quality need to be assured. Poor quality opportunities will let people down again, and another let-down will discourage further attempts.

Programmes for young people

8.3 For young people aged 16-19, a universal mechanism to help those with poor basic skills is already being put in place. Key Skills are an integral part of study for GNVQs, Modern Apprenticeships and National Traineeships, and a free-standing qualification in application of number, communication (and IT) is being piloted which will enable young people taking any post-16 route to develop these skills further. This is now a central part of the Government's 16-19 strategy for *Investing in Young People*, which aims to raise participation and attainment among 14-19 year olds in line with the National Targets.

8.4 The DfEE will soon be consulting on proposals for key elements of that strategy, including new pre-vocational provision covering outreach, assessment and guidance functions, as well as basic, key, personal and social skills. It is widely believed that people can only improve their Key Skills if, as part of this, they improve their literacy and numeracy. Therefore, in developing the *Investing in Young People* Strategy, we propose that the Government should consider ways of ensuring that:

- the proposed "gateway" for 16 and 17 year olds includes a focus on basic skills through initial assessment and pre-vocational training;
- young people aged 16 and 17 who are entitled to Time Off for Study under new legislation are identified by careers services and colleges as a priority group for targeting basic skills support;
- National Training Organisations (NTOs) and employers ensure that Modern Apprenticeships and National Traineeships include intensive basic skills support where appropriate.

8.5 We realise that the focus of Government and employers is on key skills. However, as a basis for employability, since basic skills are the foundation for this, we suggest in Chapter 10 that it is worth considering whether all Key Skills qualifications should require the achievement of a qualification in basic skills.

Programmes for the unemployed

8.6 The New Deals are well placed to provide effective basic skills provision. With New Deal 18-24, young people with basic skills needs can be offered training within the initial Gateway stage of up to four months. Basic skills training can also be undertaken after Gateway, either within the full time education and training option or as part of the training which is required for all other options. The New Deal for 25 plus, New Deal for Lone Parents and New Deal for Disabled People all offer a range of intensive and tailored advice for Jobseekers. This too can involve identifying opportunities for basic skills training where this is required.

8.7 It is essential that periods of unemployment are used to improve skills levels. The link between employability and skills levels is well known, and recent research has provided evidence that the skills levels of those with skills below Level 2 are likely to deteriorate substantially when unemployment occurs[41].

8.8 It is against this background that we make our recommendation (Recommendation 5) on the way the New Deal can be used to help in the National Strategy proposed here.

8.9 It is also important that as arrangements for the Single Work Focused Gateway are developed, benefit claimants are entitled to assessment of their basic skills and the offer of effective provision to improve their skills. Whether they take up the offer must, of course, be their own decision.

Workplace programmes

8.10 At work, basic skills matter crucially. They are a key to employability – of getting into and staying in work. They are the pre-requisite skills for the development and use of key skills that employers increasingly demand of their employees. And there is evidence that they are growing in importance, employers rate them ever more highly.

8.11 Moreover, poor basic skills affect the efficiency and competitiveness of the economy. The pace of development and change in business is undermined. They represent a significant cost to British industry.

8.12 One of the prime motivations for many adults to improve their basic skills can be their work. They join programmes to get work, to stay in work, and to be promoted and move on to other work. The purpose is to enhance their employability. However, all too few have the opportunity to learn in the workplace. The provision of more such opportunities is a key element in the National Strategy.

8.13 We start from a position where workplace provision is regrettably limited. Many employers do not see it as their responsibility to take on the improvement of basic skills. We were struck – and shocked – by this limited commitment within industry and business generally. It represents one of the most important areas for change.

8.14 Left to chance, we doubt if many more employers would get involved. We have been persuaded by our discussions and evidence that high level pressure would not convince most companies, nor would the much-needed publicity campaign or leadership from the CBI, the TUC, the TEC National Council or Chambers of Commerce. The problem goes deeper.

8.15 It is therefore important to assess:

- what would motivate employers to set up basic skills programmes for their employees? What barriers need to be overcome?
- how could employer bodies and unions stimulate the growth of workplace basic skills programmes?
- how will the new University for Industry help to develop workplace programmes in small and medium size, as well as large, companies?

8.16 Many employers feel that improving standards of literacy and numeracy is a matter for schools, that the education system has failed and that it was never their role to provide basic education. In a sense they are of course right. In due course this will hopefully be the case. But it in no way lessens their responsibility in helping today's adults. Nor have the plethora of qualifications and inadequate and confusing standards in the past encouraged employer involvement. Once the proposed strategy is being implemented, the context for employer participation will be encouraged.

8.17 Most employers are at least aware of the problem. The recent National Skills Task Force report, *Towards a National Skills Agenda*, noted that 'significant numbers of employers also said that their employees lacked basic literacy and numeracy skills'[42].

8.18 Many employers do appreciate that a grasp of basic skills is essential to employability, and for acquiring wider, and higher level, key skills. Key skills in turn are an integral part of developing vocational qualifications. But persuading the great majority of employers of the value of basic skills as part of overall training remains a major task. One problem seems to be, as the CBI has noted, that employers in general can deal with key skills, but do not have the expertise to tackle basic skills. They need help.

8.19 They need to be convinced that improving the basic skills of their workforce will help with the 'bottom line'. Waste will be reduced, productivity per employee will increase and staff turnover will fall. The "cost" to a company of poor basic skills can reasonably be at the front of employers' minds.

8.20 New mechanisms must therefore be developed to help employers to recognise, identify and tackle these needs. Employers should be able to get free advice on how to organise effective courses. This should include guidance on assessment, programme development, qualifications and achievement, and quality assurance. The example of excellent provision, such as with Ford, GKN and Glaxo-Wellcome, should be widely publicised and, hopefully, copied. To encourage employers we recommend below the establishment of a separate Workplace Basic Skills Development Fund.

8.21 A specific help would be via release from work for people with poor basic skills. Often it is the cost of cover that prevents an employer from providing basic skills support, either in the workplace or elsewhere. Clearly this must be limited because of expense and disruption. However, a Government-financed scheme to cover the wage cost of release for 1 day a week for 13 weeks (for people below Level 1) would allow people with problems to receive valuable 'booster' periods of teaching.

8.22 A key role can be played by the new National Training Organisations (NTOs). Their remit is to raise standards of education, training and development in their sector, and the development of national occupational standards, and some already recognise the importance of basic skills. We believe that all NTOs should ensure that basic skills needs in their sectors are identified and addressed in their work. The National Skills Task Force can, in its future work, support this initiative.

8.23 Companies which seek to become Investors in People have an excellent opportunity to identify the basic skills needs of employees. This standard is one of the main tools for improving business performance through the training and development of people, and a major review of the Standard is now taking place. In conducting the review, Investors in People UK, the responsible national organisation, should consider how the Standard can be revised to support basic skills at work. Current plans to strengthen the recruitment and induction process in Investors in People should include explicit advice for employers on the identification of basic skills needs, and advice on measures to tackle them.

8.24 A key question in the development of workplace basic skills is how to get more small and medium size companies (SMEs) involved. Although some do have training or personnel staff many do not. Often staff training is one of many responsibilities falling to a general manager. Increasing employer awareness through campaigns is not enough. We recommend that incentives should be introduced to help companies, particularly small and medium size companies, to introduce relevant programmes. The principle here is that a learner should be treated equally – as regards funding of programmes – whatever his or her employment status. This leads us to recommend that the Government should set up a Workplace Basic Skills Development Fund. This would provide seed funding for companies to set up basic skills programmes either in the workplace or at a local institution such as a college or adult education centre. It would provide the funding required for essential advice and guidance, the training of key staff and the costs of courses.

8.25 Amongst the other proposals set out below in Recommendation 6, there is the important proposal that training for basic skills at work should be funded on a par with funding from FE Colleges.

Trade unions

8.26 Trade unions have a long tradition of involvement in education and training, and there are many examples of successful partnerships in the public and private sector. Though the Employment Relations Bill will not give unions a right to negotiate on training, we believe that this should be promoted to employers and unions as good practice. It could significantly boost the effective involvement of unions in education and training provision in the workplace.

8.27 We know that the TUC already provides practical assistance to unions through TUC bargaining for skills projects. *The Learning Age* has also encouraged trade unions to play a strong role, and there is now a Union Learning Fund to support trade union led innovation in lifelong learning. Union-led programmes are often seen by employees as safe, credible and relevant, and therefore employers should, where possible, work closely with unions in the development of workplace provision.

8.28 Unions clearly have a central role to play in raising standards of basic skills of adults. We recommend that:

a. unions should provide basic skills programmes for their members based on the new National Strategy;

b. unions should work with the TUC to train and develop 'union learning representatives' who should support and advise learners and work with employers on the development of basic skills provision in the workplace;

c. unions should be encouraged to submit bids to the Union Learning Fund and the Workplace Basic Skills Development Fund for the development of basic skills programmes.

University for Industry

8.29 The University for Industry will bring new opportunities for companies, particularly SMEs, to boost their competitiveness and for individuals to enhance their employability. Basic skills opportunities for adults have been identified as one of the four initial priorities, which is most encouraging. In order to reach its target of reaching 200,000 basic skills learners over 3 years, the UfI will need to be active in a number of areas. We hope that it will take the lead in promoting the value and 'bottom line' benefits of basic skills programmes. It should make help with basic skills, and guidance on how to get such help, widely available.

8.30 Clearly, the UfI will reach out beyond industry and workplace. Its learning centres will draw in new groups of learners with other interests and motivations. It will develop a range of high-quality distance programmes, using the world-wide web and the power of digital TV and other technologies. This will bring the chance to learn into the home. All this will greatly encourage many new learners.

8.31 Based on the successful models of basic skills programmes, in particular the Open Learning Centres, which made successful use of new technology to stimulate learning in basic skills, we believe and hope that the University for Industry's work on basic skills will include:

- the construction of an overall framework of assessment, induction, guidance and basic skills training;
- initial and summative assessment material;
- a series of programmes that deliver training and practice in common basic and key skills required in the workplace and everyday life;
- a 'capture' facility that will allow authentic workplace materials to be inserted into and supported by basic skills programs;
- a set of basic skills learning packages accessed by learners through video or broadcast means;
- an intensive staff training package to enable basic and key skills staff to use the UfI material effectively.

8.32 With our emphasis on standards and quality in mind, we hope that the UfI will;

a. ensure that learners on UfI-endorsed courses below Level 2 have access to, and guidance on, basic skills help;

b. ensure that materials, tutor support and qualifications used in UfI-endorsed study meet the quality standards we propose;

c. commission multimedia basic skills products, on-line learning and digital TV programmes, to provide for adults with basic skills needs through learning centres and at home.

Community-based programmes

8.33 It is wrong to regard a large number of adults with poor basic skills as permanently hard to reach. Arrangements need to be made to package provision in a way that is attractive to all. The best examples of community-based provision have motivated some of those not otherwise attracted by the simple device of linking provision to common concerns.

8.34 Only by harnessing the energy and outreach of community organisations will the message of basic skills get across to large numbers in the target group. Community organisations are often close to those who are not participants in formal education or in civic life. Their contribution within the National Strategy is vital.

8.35 Such organisations operate in many spheres: in housing, crime prevention, credit unions, self-help groups, social action bodies and elsewhere. Many workers in these organisations know that their clients, members, or colleagues have basic skills difficulties, but may not have the knowledge or skills to help them.

8.36 Schools have a key role to play in increasing the opportunities available for adults to improve basic skills. Schools are central to the Government's strategy to raise standards of literacy of children and young people but this should not mean that they do not have a part to play in our National Strategy. In many communities the local school is the main resource available and, particularly in rural areas, schools are often the centre-piece of the community. Of course, some adults – with bad memories of school – will not want to relive them. However, experience –

particularly the experience of family literacy and family numeracy programmes – indicates that for some adults the local school is the most convenient venue. Population movement also means that it is now much less likely that someone attending a school-based programme actually attended the same school.

8.37 It is also worth mentioning that the Government's New Deal for Communities programme will fund comprehensive strategies to regenerate small neighbourhoods in some of the most deprived areas of the country. It will bring together local people, community and voluntary organisations, public agencies, local authorities and business in an intensive local focus to make lasting improvements. Basic skills should form an integral part of these plans.

8.38 Through its newly established Adult and Community Learning Fund, the Government has made a commitment to enable community-based organisations to help in tackling basic skills. Some 100 organisations have already been supported. The work of the Fund over the next two years will have a crucial role in funding valuable work. However, it cannot fund all that needs to be done.

8.39 We therefore think it is vital that a sizeable part of the funding made available for the proposed Local Partnership Action Plans should be devoted to community-based basic skills work. The adequacy of what is proposed should be a factor in the Secretary of State's decision in approving the plans.

Basic skills support in colleges

8.40 The National Strategy envisages a major expansion of initial assessment in colleges and of basic skills support programmes, and we recommend that by 2002:

a all colleges in the further education sector should be required to assess all appropriate[43] students enrolling in the college and that this initial assessment and offer of additional support is a requirement of funding;

b. initial assessment should be part of the college/student 'contract'.

Literacy and numeracy courses

8.41 We have already expressed our view that more, and more diverse, literacy and numeracy courses for adults need to be made available. The current level of provision will not accommodate the additional learners envisaged in *The Learning Age* target, let alone our proposed targets. Nor is it just a matter of providing more of what exists now. If new groups of adults are to be attracted, the range of opportunities needs to change radically. We must ensure diversity.

8.42 The changes needed can be summarised as follows:

- an increase in the number of full-time courses to enable adults to gain skills more quickly;
- shorter intensive 'booster' courses, including weekend, and residential and non-residential summer school courses;

- more open learning provision, through drop-in centres linked to the UfI;
- an increase in specialist individual help, outside normal learning centres and at times to suit adults with specific needs;
- greater targeting of provision, including specific programmes, to ensure that adults get substantial help to meet immediate needs.

Family-based programmes

8.43 Family literacy and family numeracy programmes are very effective in attracting parents. They help to prevent early failure in young children and improve the literacy and numeracy skills of adults.

8.44 These programmes have been expanded in the last few years primarily through specific funding as part of the Standards Fund. It is important for this expansion to continue and eventually for all infant and primary schools in areas with greatest need to have a family literacy and family numeracy programme.

8.45 We also want to see further exploration of effective models of family literacy and family numeracy. Different models are required for different circumstances. For example, we were impressed by the family basic skills programmes based in Ford in Dagenham, and feel that more employers need to provide similar programmes for workers and their families. The active involvement of trade unions will help in attracting families.

8.46 Whatever new models are developed will need to be rigorously evaluated. Resources are too scarce for trial and error, and we cannot afford to encourage expenditure on programmes that may not work effectively. The Basic Skills Agency should continue to develop and evaluate new approaches in this area.

RECOMMENDATION 5 – Programmes for the Unemployed

(i) The Government should:

(a) ensure that the basic skills of all New Deal clients are assessed soon after they make contact with their Personal Adviser, and that intensive basic skills courses are offered early on to those with basic skills at Entry Level or below;

(b) ensure that all claimants for benefit are entitled to assessment of basic skills and offered effective provision to improve their skills if below Level 2.

(ii) The New Deal Task Force should be asked urgently to ensure that clients with basic skills below Level 2, on options other than the education and training option, get access to basic skills support.

(iii) Training should be provided for all Personal Advisers so that they can identify basic skills needs and encourage the take-up of basic skills opportunities where this is necessary.

RECOMMENDATION 6 – Workplace Programmes

(i) The Government should set up a Workplace Basic Skills Development Fund. This would provide seed funding for companies to set up basic skills programmes either in the workplace or at a local institution such as a college or adult education centre.

(ii) Up to a fixed budget limit, the Government should finance the wage cost of day release for up to 13 weeks for people with basic skills below Level 1.

(iii) The revised *Investors in People* guidance should include a requirement for companies to have effective arrangements for assessing and dealing with basic skills difficulties.

(iv) Training for basic skills at the workplace should be funded on a par with funding of such programmes in FE Colleges.

(v) A 'pledge' scheme for companies should be introduced to allow them to indicate their support for raising standards of basic skills among adults.

RECOMMENDATION 7 – Trade Unions

(i) Unions should provide basic skills programmes for their members based on the new National Strategy

(ii) Unions should work with the TUC to train and develop "union learning representatives", who would support and advise learners and work with employers on the development of basic skills provision in the workplace.

(iii) Unions should be encouraged to submit bids to the Union Learning Fund, and the Workplace Basic Skills Development Fund, for the development of basic skills programmes.

RECOMMENDATION 8 – The University for Industry

In pursuing its commitment to making basic skills a priority, the UfI should:

(i) ensure that learners undertaking courses below Level 2 through UfI-endorsed programmes should have access to, and guidance on, basic skills help available;

(ii) ensure that in working towards its targets for basic skills support in the workplace and elsewhere, materials, tutor support and qualifications meet the quality standards we propose;

(iii) commission multimedia basic skills products, on-line learning and digital TV programmes, to provide for adults with basic skills needs through learning centres and at home.

RECOMMENDATION 9 – Community-Based Programmes

Local Basic Skills Action Plans should specifically include community-based provision to meet increased local need, for which particular resources should be identified. The Secretary of State should take account of the adequacy of such community-based provision in approving local Adult Basic Skills Action Plans.

RECOMMENDATION 10 – Basic Skills Support in Colleges

(i) As soon as possible, and no later than 2002, all providers funded by FEFC should, as a requirement of funding, be required to assess all appropriate students enrolling and offer additional support.

(ii) By 2002 all students assessed as requiring additional support with basic skills in colleges should be able to take up this help.

RECOMMENDATION 11 – Family-Based Programmes

(i) All infant and primary schools in educationally disadvantaged areas should have family literacy and numeracy programmes by 2002.

(ii) The Basic Skills Agency should continue to develop and evaluate new models of family literacy and family numeracy programmes.

Part 3

Our Strategy

Chapter 9: Quality

Effective programmes

9.1 Every bit as important as diversity of opportunity is that the standard of what is on offer is uniformly and dependably high. High-quality provision is a positive encouragement, not least to people who have experienced failure earlier in their educational lives. Poor quality of courses or teaching would be another discouragement.

9.2 It is evident from key sources, including the three inspection agencies, that there is much to improve in what is on offer. Nevertheless, evidence presented to us has provided valuable information on what is most effective in enabling adults to improve their basic skills. Some of this evidence is published separately by the Basic Skills Agency in *Effective Basic Skills Provision for Adults* which describes the elements of effective provision. In future, all basic skills teaching programmes funded from the public purse through Local Partnerships should include these elements.

9.3 Some of the hallmarks of good quality teaching are programmes that:

- deliver clearly structured teaching in literacy and numeracy;
- provide for the acquisition of skills in a range of contexts that meet the motivation and interests of learners;
- have high expectations of learners' achievements;
- produce for each learner a learning plan that lists and provides activities and material to meet specified individual need;
- regularly assess and review learner progress, and adjust individual learning plans accordingly;
- enable learners to gain credit and accreditation for their learning and enable them to study further;

- adjust the length of programme according to the level of skills required.

9.4 In order to end the patchiness of the current position, a common framework of standards is required for all programmes, standards that will hold good across the range of programmes, funders and inspection regimes. Only through such a coherent framework can an effective and coordinated strategy be ensured.

9.5 We referred in Chapter 4 to the problems of the present inspection arrangements. It is crucial that the three inspection agencies work together on a common and strengthened inspection framework. This should be based on clear and transparent criteria, ensuring that everyone involved – the inspection agencies, colleges and indeed all providers – are clear about what is expected from them and what they will be inspected on.

9.6 The Basic Skills Agency Quality Mark for Post-16 Programmes is a good example of how basic skills programmes can become more effective. It is matched by a similar Quality Mark for primary schools and secondary schools. The post-16 Quality Mark is based on 10 elements.

9.7 *The Learning Age* recognised the importance of quality in lifelong learning and proposed that 'the Basic Skills Agency, the FEFC Inspectorate and OFSTED work together, and with such others as the Training Standards Inspectorate, to improve literacy and numeracy provision. This will include the use of the Basic Skills Agency's Quality Mark, and the use of benchmarks, targets and performance indicators, as well as reviewing standards of teaching and the use of materials'. We support this proposal.

Effective teachers

9.8 We are conscious of the devoted and effective work of many of those now teaching basic skills, including the many volunteers, yet the proposed strategy will need:

- far more well-trained teachers;
- an appropriate balance between full and part-time staff;
- specifically-trained staff who have regular opportunities for up-dating their knowledge and skills;

1. A strategy, including a written action plan, to improve standards of basic skills
2. An estimate of the scale of need for help with basic skills in the area covered by the programme
3. Targets for the improvement in performance in basic skills
4. A negotiated learning plan for each learner
5. A regular review of progress
6. Access to the nationally recognised qualification in basic skills
7. Teaching by trained and qualified staff
8. The use of a range of teaching styles to improve basic skills
9. The use of appropriate teaching and learning material to improve basic skills
10. An effective procedure for monitoring the action plan and assessing improvement in effectiveness

- trained teachers that can teach in a variety of contexts;
- a procedure for selecting, training and supporting volunteers.

9.9 We estimate that ultimately some 15,000 full-time equivalent teachers will be required, compared with under 4,000 at present.

9.10 The present balance of full-time and part-time staff is not appropriate. Currently less than 1 in 10 of the staff working on these adult programmes is full-time, and more than 1 in 3 are employed for less than 6 hours a week. Though the part played by part-time staff is vital, we need to find ways of bringing in a greater full-time teaching force.

9.11 In programmes operating with large numbers of part-time staff working 2-4 hours a week, the effectiveness of teaching is limited. There is almost bound to be a lack of consistency in teaching methods and the fact that part-time teachers receive little continuous professional development is an added disadvantage.

9.12 We propose that each Partnership should include in its Action Plan details of how it intends to move towards a better balance between full and part-time staff, including volunteers. Flexibility is important and we do not wish to recommend a precise balance. But nationally the aim should be that something like half of those teaching should be full-time.

9.13 Training is crucial. There is evidence that programmes using well-trained staff, who receive regular professional up-dating, achieve the best outcomes in terms of learner achievements[44]. As we noted in an earlier chapter, the FEFC's recent report on Programme Area 10 has commented on this problem, suggesting that basic education staff frequently have no relevant qualification for the area in which they teach.

9.14 Staff working in specific contexts should be trained specifically for these contexts. For example, in programmes for unemployed people, a vocational focus is crucial. Staff must be able to analyse jobs into their component tasks, identifying the literacy and numeracy requirements. In the case of foundation training or dedicated provision, staff may need to acquire familiarity with a wide range of job tasks, in order to keep work and related literacy and numeracy demands at the centre. Similarly, staff providing training at the workplace require the skills needed to teach basic skills in that particular context.

9.15 Some community-based programmes have been successful in training staff to teach basic skills in the specific context of their client group[45]. For example, London Connection, a project working with homeless young people, has provided training for a number of members of existing staff so that they are able to identify and support basic skills needs if they arise, and are able to do so within the context of the individual's wider needs[46].

9.16 Progress has been made in developing appropriate qualifications for teachers of basic skills to adults. The Basic Skills Agency introduced initial accredited training in 1991 and more demanding in-service training in 1993. Before that, little teacher accreditation existed. However, more demanding accreditation is required.

9.17 The solution is to develop more demanding initial training as a compulsory preparation for new staff and volunteers in adult programmes. The BSA and the new Further Education National Training Organisation (FENTO) should work together to produce such qualifications, in collaboration with the national awarding bodies. We would also like to see diploma courses established in University Education Departments.

9.18 Such developments need careful preparation and will take time to become reality. Yet, given the importance of improvement, we want to follow the model of the National Literacy Strategy, and propose that intensive courses be introduced urgently for key staff to help in implementing the new core curriculum.

Effective teaching

9.19 The quality of teaching is one of the most important factors in influencing whether someone learns well and effectively. There is no single effective teaching style suitable for all learners, and we would expect to see a range of approaches in use, including whole class teaching, small group work and individual instruction.

9.20 Every learner in a basic skills programme should have a written study plan, agreed with tutors and teachers. Such a plan should:

- be negotiated and agreed between the programme and the learner;
- include specific targets and learning goals;
- contain an outline of the steps needed to reach a particular goal;
- include details of the skills and knowledge being developed;
- be reviewed and revised regularly.

9.21 It is important to ensure that there is an appropriate[47] staff/learner ratio in teaching groups, hopefully allowing for some individual attention. Otherwise drop-out rates will go up and learners may make little progress.

9.22 It is more difficult to establish ratios for learning support where learners attend a workshop or centre, have a large element of self-study and make use of new technology. However, what is important in these circumstances is for learners to have individual specialist advice and support from staff.

9.23 Teaching always needs to take account of the context for learning. So, for example, teaching on workplace courses or on family literacy programmes needs to relate to the main purpose a learner has for wanting to improve basic skills.

9.24 All learners should have access to appropriate learning material; material that is varied, helpful in improving specific skills and knowledge and is relevant to the learners' age, interests and abilities. Material should:

- be appropriate for specific age groups;
- provide an adequate level of guidance as to how they are used and for what purpose, to teach which specific skills, within a range of activities;
- give regular test, assessment and feedback information, both to the teacher and the learner;
- be structured to ensure clear progression in levels within texts;
- be contextualised, while retaining clear focus on underpinning skills.

9.25 Very little existing material is targeted at workplace learning. Effective workplace programmes have used generic material for the teaching of these skills. However, applying these skills to the context of work, and providing the contextualised practice material that both employees and employers value, requires vocationally specific material. This is a gap that needs to be filled.

The benefits of new technology

9.26 At the heart of improved quality in delivery and materials must be increased use of Information and Communication Technologies (ICT) to improve basic skills. There are a number of reasons why this is an important element for the future.

9.27 Firstly, ICT provides a powerful motivation for adults with poor basic skills. Few will have used computers or related technology at school. It does not therefore evoke the memories of struggle and failure that paper, pencil and books often recall. A computer can also enable a learner to be a more successful writer, more quickly: to produce letters and other writing that looks good, without crossings out, poor handwriting or a number of paper drafts.

9.28 Secondly, learners who use ICT for basic skills increase the value of their study time. They acquire keyboard and other computing skills as they improve their reading, writing or maths. Open Learning Centres used this twin track approach effectively, drawing new groups of adults into programmes that enabled them to gain qualifications in using computers, as well as in basic skills.

9.29 Thirdly, the power of the new technologies can enable teachers to provide methods of learning less possible with print materials. For example:

- the availability of sound is an important empowering tool: it enables learners to check the accuracy of their reading independently; text-to-speech and speech-to-text technologies speed the process of comprehension and composition;
- multimedia programmes have the flexibility to produce material that is quickly made useful for the individual learner, for example to a specific work context or industrial sector.

9.30 Fourthly, the World-Wide Web and digital television offer new ways to reach adults with poor basic skills and to encourage them to learn. They open up the prospect of providing learners with what they say that they want, high-quality home-supported programmes.

9.31 Fifthly, ICT has been a key factor in convincing employers to invest in basic skills training. The introduction of ICT into the workplace has often provided the spark for identifying employees' basic skills needs, and calling in experts to provide training.

9.32 Recent Australian research[48] found that the use of ICT led to 'increased output, a greater understanding of what producing written text involves, increased participation by learners and higher levels of enthusiasm and interest'. We were also impressed to learn about initiatives in the USA to develop the use of technology to improve basic skills[49].

9.33 So ICT should increasingly be part of all basic skills teaching and study programmes. However, there are key issues that must be resolved:

- basic skills learners need ready access to modern computers and other technology, including the Web;
- there must be an improved range of software programs suitable for adult basic skills users, with clear quality criteria for their content and use;
- programmes need staff skilled and knowledgeable in the best use of ICT.

9.34 Recent surveys[50] have identified a need for a greater number and higher capacity computers for use in basic skills programmes. If we are to see a substantial improvement in the quality of programmes the upgrade and increase of computers available to basic skills students should be a high priority for colleges and other basic skills providers. We welcome the recent initative by the DfEE of making available over £4 million worth of high quality hardware to adult education and community based programmes. This is an important first step.

9.35 Elsewhere we describe the important role that the University for Industry (UfI) can play in attracting new basic skills learners. The UfI must also ensure that there is an adequate range of learning styles using the new technologies. This will include on-line learning in traditional programmes, the choice to learn in new UfI learning centres, and learning at home.

9.36 But other players must be drawn in. The new National Grid for Learning (NGFL) provides a powerful resource. It is the information highway that connects schools across the country, and will be the source for new materials and new ways of learning. Already it supports the Literacy and Numeracy Strategies for Schools. But we believe that the NGFL can be harnessed to support adult basic skills learning, through out of school hours programmes that involve parents and other adults.

9.37 There are a small number of good software programs that have been produced for adult basic skills teaching. Recent multimedia CD-ROMs have improved the quality of what learners can use, in addition to generic word-processing, spreadsheet and database packages. However, there must be more, including:

- on-line initial and ongoing assessment;
- programs that make use of the technology available to develop a range of reading, writing, spelling and numeracy skills;
- language fluency programs;
- distance teacher support.

9.38 Schools and FE colleges are making increasing use of new learning programmes, such as Integrated Learning Systems (ILS). These products provide a course of instruction in literacy and numeracy, practice on what has been learnt and assessment of performance through tests. Despite the inconclusive results of research by the British Educational and Communications Technology Agency (BECTa) into the effectiveness of ILS, it is nevertheless a tool that must be further explored for its relevance to adults.

9.39 Digital TV is a new medium. Few households have the televisions or set-top boxes to access digital TV. However, usage is growing rapidly. And perhaps more significantly, digital TV sales are reported to be greater amongst social groups and classes where basic skills needs are greater. Led by sport, home movies and home shopping, digital TV is set to achieve the kind of reach that we believe is necessary to get home learning of basic skills established. Digital teletext, introduced later in 1999, offers the prime medium for this development. Early development of basic skills digital material is under way, led by the Basic Skills Agency and partners in the Upgrade ESF project, and the Digital College in Wales.

9.40 As the usage of ICT in basic skills provision increases, so will the need for well-trained staff who know how to use it. Previous evaluation of computer-based initiatives has pointed to the lack of confidence of staff as a barrier to effective use. We believe, therefore, that training in this area is a priority for basic skills staff.

9.41 As for Information Technology as a basic skill in itself, we welcome the intention of the National Skills Task Force to examine the question of IT literacy in its work on key skills and employability.

RECOMMENDATION 12 –Quality Assurance

By 2002 all basic skills programmes should be required to meet a new nationally determined framework of standards in order to qualify for funding.

RECOMMENDATION 13 – Inspection

The three inspection agencies, FEFC, OFSTED and TSC, should work together on a common inspection framework based on clear and transparent standards and consistent with the proposed national quality framework.

RECOMMENDATION 14 – Teacher Training

(i) All new staff and volunteers should undertake recognised initial training in teaching literacy and numeracy to adults.

(ii) The BSA, the new Further Education National Training Organisation (FENTO) and others should work together to produce new qualifications for teaching basic skills to adults.

(iii) By 2005 all teachers of basic skills should have this qualification or an equivalent.

(iv) Diploma courses in teaching basic skills to adults should be established in University Education Departments.

(v) Intensive courses for teachers to become familiar with the new curriculum should be mounted.

RECOMMENDATION 15 – Use of Information and Communication Technologies

In view of the importance of Information and Communication Technology in basic skill learning programmes, the DfEE should ensure, in collaboration with relevant bodies, that such programmes receive all the necessary advice and support.

Chapter 10: A New Basic Skills Curriculum and a New System of Qualifications

A new basic skills curriculum

10.1 One of the crucial elements of the proposed strategy must be clarity about the skills, knowledge and understanding that anyone needs to be literate and numerate in the modern world. These skills need to be enshrined in a new curriculum, with well-developed and understood standards.

10.2 At present the position is somewhat like that for schools before the introduction of the National Curriculum. Teachers do teach much the same skills whatever the context, and wherever they work. But there is no coherent, publicly available, written curriculum covering all basic skills teaching programmes. What is needed is a curriculum which makes clear what specific skills need to be learned and taught. Alongside this, there should be a new system of qualifications based on the curriculum. Without a mandatory curriculum, learners may leave programmes without the skills they need to be competent and confident in essential basic skills.

10.3 The proposed curriculum should set out, in a logical order, the literacy and numeracy skills every adult needs. Although there will be similarities between this and the National Curriculum for schools, there are some clear differences. For example, much of the English National Curriculum in schools is, rightly, about what is read rather than about the skills needed for fluent reading.

10.4 There are major differences between curricula for adults and children. For both, clear frameworks are needed, but in the case of adults, the background and starting point is a key factor. Adults bring differing experience and knowledge to the process of learning and study. And, unlike children in primary school, adults often look back to earlier attempts to acquire basic skills, and perhaps of failing in their efforts. Some may have been taught using a particular approach, such as breakthrough, a phonic only method, and so forth. Others may have missed critical periods of schooling through illness, or may have had learning problems, or were simply left behind in class.

10.5 In general both children and adults become good readers by using a range of learning approaches, not necessarily struggling with one method. Teachers need to be prepared to use a range of techniques. In all, the standard curriculum will be the uniform base.

10.6 This is not the place to set out the details of the curriculum we have in mind, but the examples provided below indicate the approach.

10.7 The new basic skills curriculum must operate at three levels. It will describe basic skills at Entry Level, Level 1 and Level 2. The curriculum would include:

- a description of the range of reading, writing, speaking/listening and numeracy skills that apply to each level; and
- a list of the discrete skills and knowledge requirements.

10.8 For example, at Entry Level, the development of reading skills will encompass:

Range

Narrative	stories, accounts with predictable structures, familiar language within the learners experience, language experience texts, simple graded readers within the learner's ability, simple readers, simplified newspaper articles
Non fiction	signs, symbols, basic instructions, notes, messages

Skills and Knowledge

Word Level

Word recognition, graphic recognition

- Own name and address
- Key sight vocabulary
- Dolch list of 100 common words
- Key words in work, home or personal context (e.g. canteen, technical, etc)
- Months/days
- Numbers 1-100
- Words for basic instructions
- Key question words
- Common abbreviations (Mrs. Dr., Rd.)

Phonic and word structure

- Knowledge of the alphabet
- Grapheme/phoneme correspondence
- Knowledge of vowels and consonants
- Initial sounds
- CVC words
- Adding 's' to make plurals
- Root words with simple suffixes (-ed, -ing)
- Syllables

Sentence Level

- Prediction skills
- Sequencing
- Context cues
- Use of grammar and punctuation as an aide to comprehension

Text Level

- Comprehension of text
- Upper and lower case correspondence
- Read and use captions
- Scan for specific meaning
- Read charts, diagrams, tables

10.9 In addition to the levels, range and skills, there should be exemplar activities to support each of the elements of the curriculum. These skills and activities will then be drawn together into a number of integrated tasks that demonstrate both knowledge and application. For example, in literacy:

Literacy

Basic Skills Curriculum Elements	Activities
• Alphabet	• Find given words in an alphabetical list
• Scanning	• Scan paragraph for personal vocabulary/find target phrase in a page of text
• Social sight	• Sort key words and social sight words in alphabet order
• Prediction and cloze procedure	• Guess key words from context
• Dolch list	• Fill in missing words
• Grapheme/phoneme correspondence	• Recognise words from shape and sound
• Comprehension	• Follow written instructions correctly

Integrated Tasks

- Find given supplier in a directory
- Correctly complete the appropriate parts of an accident form
- Draw a simple map with instructions to help find the toilets
- Proof a letter for spelling mistakes
- Design an accident reporting form against given criteria
- Identify and classify jobs from advertisements
- Find a selection of books in a library
- Lay out self-assembly items following written instructions

10.10 As far as possible, the proposed curriculum for adults should be "context free". The core should set out the skills to be taught. The context in which they are taught is a matter for the teacher and learner to decide, particularly as different adults have different motivations. In short, the curriculum is not a series of rigid lesson plans to be taught by every teacher and followed by every learner. Adults will be encouraged, and hopefully excited, by reading a wide range of texts in a wide range of contexts. The range and nature of materials for a family literacy programme will differ from that for a trainee in a workplace programme. Learners should be able to develop the skills common to them all, using the interests, the materials and the activities that most closely match their needs.

A new system of qualifications

10.11 Although many adult learners use basic skills courses for personal satisfaction or to equip themselves for courses leading to mainstream qualifications such as GCSE and A Level, others want certification of their achievements. We propose qualifications that certify possession of literacy and numeracy skills in accordance with agreed national standards, as set out in the new national curriculum.

10.12 At present there are too many qualifications available in literacy and numeracy for adults. The FEFC, for instance, provides funding for 60 qualifications of this type. This is confusing and unhelpful. We need to know what someone with a particular qualification can actually do, what level of literacy and numeracy has been reached. This is vital for the learner, and vital to ensure credibility for employers. Existing qualifications often lack credibility; many employers do not accept them and use their own tests. So we propose that the FEFC, TECs and other funding bodies should recognise for funding only those qualifications based on skills set out in the new curriculum.

10.13 We recommend a new system of qualifications based on the skills set out in this curriculum. As the National Strategies to improve school performance take effect the problem with adults will diminish, and in time even the new qualifications may prove to be redundant. But this is far off in the future, and for some time ahead there is a clear need to incorporate in the National Strategy a new system of qualifications.

Criteria

10.14 Qualifications serve five purposes:

a. they provide a goal for learners;

b. they provide feedback to teachers telling them whether teaching aims have been achieved;

c. they provide evidence for employers and educational institutions that national standards have been achieved;

d. they give information to funders which can be used in their choice of providers and in their funding arrangements;

e. they give information on the extent of low literacy and numeracy and the effectiveness of programmes to improve literacy and numeracy standards.

10.15 In sum, the system must have three vital characteristics – credibility, ease of access and an incentive for learners.

10.16 **Credibility** – The system of qualifications must give a reliable measure of an individual's skill. It must certify to those who wish to use the qualification (learners, employers, educational institutions etc.) that skills matching national standards have been acquired. It will provide a benchmark of how well providers of courses are doing, and – as qualifications become more credible – employers will value them more and potential learners will want them more.

10.17 **Ease of access** – Many adults want to improve their literacy and numeracy without doing a formal course. They may have fairly minor weaknesses and can deal with them without formal teaching or through distance learning and the University for Industry. Information technology will be of crucial help to them at work, at home or elsewhere. In any case, it should always be possible to get a qualification without attending a course. At the same time, one must bear in mind that many potential learners, especially if they have serious problems, may want face-to-face teaching. The curricula, qualifications and standards should apply at all levels and to all learners. And at each level they should be obtainable through the accumulation of credits in separate components of the curriculum. It must be possible to get these credits whenever the learner wants to, and in 'bite-size' chunks, or modules.

10.18 **Incentive for learners** – The new qualifications must be such as to motivate learners, to boost confidence and self-esteem. People should want them. Even the best qualification will be useless if the potential learners – the people whose needs we have tried to make centre stage – do not want to gain them.

10.19 As regards the methods of assessment to be used in leading to the qualifications, two methods are used at present: a 'portfolio' based on coursework assessment, which may include test results, and externally set and marked tests.

10.20 The majority of existing basic skills qualifications are awarded through the assessment of coursework. Almost always, assessment is externally moderated. The most popular qualification of this type is Wordpower for literacy and Numberpower for numeracy. They are moderated externally by City & Guilds and the London Chamber of Commerce and Industry. In 1997, roughly 30,000 learners were studying for Wordpower and a similar number for Numberpower.

10.21 Another common delivery system based on coursework is available through Open College Credits. Providers design their own curriculum and get it accredited by the Open College Network. Much of the provision under this heading started off as providing access routes to higher education, but increasingly it has been taken up by learners operating at the most elementary education levels. Many of them take Foundation (Entry Level) courses with strong basic skills components, including English as an Additional Language. In 1997, the London Open College Credit Network was registering some 30,000 learners for credit, almost one fifth of whom were at Entry Level.

10.22 A different form of qualification is that based exclusively on tests that are externally set and marked. The most common are the Associated Examining Board (AEB) tests in Literacy and Numeracy. In 1997 almost 30,000 learners were entered for the literacy tests and a similar number entered for the numeracy tests.

The way forward

10.23 Both portfolio and test-based methods of assessment have their strengths and weaknesses. Coursework assessment is attractive to learners who would be put off by having to take a test. Also, teachers can use the assessment as a feedback to students, which can help to motivate. On the other hand, with coursework it may be harder to ensure uniform standards.

10.24 Tests have the advantage of greater objectivity, and are often thought to lead to greater credibility with employers and others. They are also attractive to adults who cannot, or do not want to, attend regular face-to-face classes.

10.25 All methods of assessment are open to abuse and some have been abused in the past. The funding methodology of various funding bodies has over-encouraged programme providers to get people through the qualification. Coaching – or insufficiently rigorous standards in assessment of coursework – has been a problem. Similarly some programmes have 'taught the test', people have sometimes passed specific entry tests for very specific occupations in this inadequate way.

10.26 In the proposed system, all qualifications offered at Entry Level and Level 1 will be based on the proposed new curriculum. For qualifications to be credible, they have to inspire confidence that the skills they certify have been acquired. This is why any external moderation needs to be rigorously applied, in accordance with national standards. External tests similarly need to be standardised.

10.27 Existing coursework-assessed qualifications can continue to be offered as long as they are based on the skills enshrined in the new curriculum. They will continue to go under a variety of names, but will in future make clear, perhaps through a simple logo, that they are nationally recognised. They can continue to be offered by a number of awarding bodies.

10.28 Alongside, we recommend the introduction of a new National Literacy Test and a new National Numeracy Test at Level 1 and Level 2. These will allow adults to demonstrate, through the passing of a test, that they have acquired the basic skills by means of a single test-assessed qualification available on demand. Whenever learners are ready, the teacher could arrange for them to sit the test. Individuals should also be able to enter at any centre operating a proper system of invigilation. In due course the UfI might provide the tests on-line. There should be only one national test, also available in 'bite-size' chunks.

10.29 Although the focus of our report, and the targets we have proposed, is the achievement of Level 1, we envisage that the new test will also apply to Level 2. There should be an opportunity for adults who wish to demonstrate that they have achieved Level 2 basic skills. Many of these will not have attended formal basic skills programmes, but will learn at home, at work or through a friend or relative. The option to take a test at Level 2 should be available to them.

10.30 The new set of qualifications would be self-standing, and it is worth considering whether qualifications in literacy and numeracy should be required elements in the Key Skills qualifications at the corresponding level, unless people have at least grade C in the relevant GCSE.

10.31 The recommendation we make on curricula and qualifications should bring about a credible framework within the proposed National Strategy. The key concept is a new curriculum, and rigorous standards to determine and demonstrate that people really have the required skills.

RECOMMENDATION 16 – Curriculum and Qualifications

(i) There should be a new national basic skills curriculum for adults, with well-defined standards of skill at Entry Level, Level 1 and Level 2.

(ii) Only basic skills qualifications based on this new curriculum should be funded from the public purse. Whether assessed by coursework, test or a mixture of both they should use a common set of standards laid down by QCA.

(iii) Existing qualifications should be revised to meet these new national standards.

(iv) Existing qualifications based exclusively on tests should be replaced by a new National Literacy Test and a new National Numeracy Test both available at Levels 1 and 2.

Chapter 11: Delivery of the Strategy – Local Partnerships

11.1 We now turn to the means by which the proposed strategy should become reality. To this end, we welcome the establishment by the Department for Education and Employment of Lifelong Learning Partnerships, which will set the context for many of our proposals. The new partnerships will provide the mechanism for the action that is required to widen participation and to identify and address gaps in provision. They will work to increase attainment and improve standards at all levels by driving action to achieve local targets, linked to the new National Learning Targets.

11.2 However, given the scale of the basic skills issue, its crucial position as a foundation for lifelong learning, and the need for a national crusade to improve basic skills, it is vital that the Partnerships should have a basic skills remit. Each Partnership should be required to produce a three-year Basic Skills Action Plan, tightly focused on meeting specific aims and achieving agreed targets. This plan would ensure that attention to this issue would be prominent in all Lifelong Learning Partnerships. Indeed, as all the other lifelong plans ultimately assume that basic skills are being improved, this is a sensible starting point for the Partnerships. We recommend that the Action Plans should be submitted directly to the Secretary of State. We also see the partnerships as the conduit through which FEFC funding would reach basic skills providers.

11.3 The Action Plans would need to include:

- an estimate of the number of people over the age of 16 years with poor basic skills in the area;[51]
- a target to reduce the estimated scale of need in its area[52], this being a direct contribution towards achieving national targets;
- a target for participation in basic skills programmes, including information on how the target would be reached;
- a description of the range of programmes that would be provided through the Partnership, based on an analysis of the diversity required to meet local needs;[53]
- any 'experimental programmes' the Partnership wish to promote;
- performance against the quality standards set out in the National Strategy;
- monitoring in each element of the programme;
- information about the coordination of the work of the Partnership.

11.4 The Action Plans should be supplemented by annual operational programmes setting out what the Partnership aims to achieve in that year. These annual programmes will allow new partners to join the local partnership.

11.5 Each Partnership will need to work to a carefully prepared and rigorous Action Plan to raise standards of adult basic skills. The Partnership will be accountable for promotion and delivery of the programmes in accordance with the National Strategy and the local targets. Future public funding for basic skills provision for adults should be geared to the Action Plans.

11.6 Partnerships will require national support in developing their Action Plans, including advice and guidance and better dissemination of effective practice. The Basic Skills Agency will have an important role to play in this, as detailed in Chapter 12.

11.7 The leadership of Lifelong Learning Partnerships is an important issue. We would not wish to be prescriptive in recommending a preferred guide. In some areas, existing partnerships with shared leadership will work well; in others they may not. In some circumstances the LEA or the TEC is the natural leader. Elsewhere, chairmanship of the partnership by a minority stakeholder ensures creative tension. What is clear is that each Partnership needs to accept responsibility for raising standards in the area they cover.

11.8 Each Partnership should set up a basic skills unit to be responsible for planning and coordination. This unit would identify bottle-necks and problems, deal with them rapidly and ensure that all the partners remained actively committed. The unit should evaluate the effectiveness of the Action Plan, and report annually to the Basic Skills Agency on progress made, and on problems that need to be addressed. The Agency will then advise the Secretary of State. This last is a crucial task, ensuring that progress – or lack of it – in every sector of the local plan is regularly evaluated, not least for cost effectiveness. The Partnership must be accountable both for the performance of providers against their adult basic skills targets and in respect of its own Action Plans. The progress made by Partnerships would be monitored.

11.9 In most cases, the partners responsible for developing the Basic Skills Action Plan will be coterminous with those involved in Lifelong Learning Partnerships. However, it is important to ensure that the key organisations, groups and individuals able to contribute to the development of basic skills provision in local communities should be involved in developing the Action Plan.

11.10 In short, the implementation of the National Strategy at local level should be the responsibility of local Lifelong Learning Partnerships. These Partnerships would include representatives of those concerned with adult basic skills. Guidance on the composition of Partnerships for the purpose of the Basic Skills Action Plan would be provided by the Secretary of State.

11.11 We endorse the advice set out in the Lifelong Learning Partnerships Remit that Partnerships should be encouraged to think creatively about whom to involve and how to structure themselves. If participation in basic skills is to be maximised with diversity of provision to meet all needs, it is essential that a wide range of organisations are involved. This will obviously include all those involved at present, but groups that might come into action in future should also be included, for example: public and private sector companies; trade unions; the library service; training organisations; agencies working in health, housing, crime prevention, social, economic and community regeneration; grassroots community groups; organisations working with specific groups, such as young people, those with learning difficulties and disabilities and dyslexic adults; prison education contractors; the careers service; and the employment service. Partnerships in areas where the needs of linguistic minority communities are significant would include community-based organisations including welfare associations, mosques and temples.

11.12 Although the focus for action should be at local level, Action Plans must feed into policy and action in the region as a whole. From April 1999 the new Regional Development Agencies will, among other things, have responsibility for developing skills plans for their regions. The need and provision for basic skills will no doubt form part of these plans. We would expect local Partnerships to take account of these in formulating their own basic skills action plans.

11.13 For obvious reasons, the work of the Government's Social Exclusion Unit is important in relation to the proposed National Strategy. The pilot schemes being undertaken by the Skills Policy Action Team – in four areas – will make a significant input to the implementation of the Strategy.

RECOMMENDATION 17 – Local Partnerships and Action Plans

(i) Implementing the National Strategy locally should be the responsibility of the local Lifelong Learning Partnerships. These would include representatives of those concerned with adult basic skills. Their composition would be submitted to the Secretary of State for guidance.

(ii) Each Partnership should be required to submit an Action Plan for the approval of the Secretary of State.

Chapter 12: National Coordination

12.1 It will be clear from the previous chapters that implementation of the National Strategy requires nation-wide efforts. The Department for Education and Employment must have the lead responsibility, but other government departments will have important roles to play. And many other institutions will need to be involved, such as educational institutions and training organisations, companies, unions, community groups, voluntary organisations and the media. Coherence and coordination will be needed nationally and locally.

12.2 If the National Strategy is to be successful, a number of functions must be performed at national level, such as:

- target-setting and leadership;
- coordination of funding;
- monitoring and development of the overall strategy;
- monitoring of action at local level towards national targets;
- promotion of the strategy;
- best practice and quality assurance advice and support for local actors;
- clear and coherent inspection.

12.3 The Secretary of State for Education and Employment will determine the National Strategy and the national targets. To help in this task, we recommend that a new National Adult Basic Skills Strategy Group, under Ministerial chairmanship, should be established by the Secretary of State. This Group, similar to the National Literacy and Numeracy Steering Group, will oversee the implementation of the National Strategy. As the strategy develops, the Group will assess progress and advise on changes or modifications. Membership would be drawn from the lead organisations involved in basic skills work with adults, and will include independent members drawn from other sectors, including community and voluntary organisations and groups and learners themselves.

12.4 As a great deal of detail will be involved, we recommend further that there should, under the main group, be a Technical Implementation Sub-Committee.

12.5 Operationally a number of functions will have to be undertaken. Our recommendations indicate which bodies and organisations should be responsible for specific tasks. For example:

- the Qualifications and Curriculum Authority, the DfEE's Standards and Effectiveness Unit and the BSA should work together to develop a new curriculum for basic skills and new basic skills qualifications;
- the new FENTO, the BSA and others should work together to produce new qualifications for basic skills teachers.

Our proposals on the allocation of responsibilities are set out in the Implementation Plan below.

12.6 Other functions that should be undertaken nationally are:

- providing advice on the composition and likely effectiveness of the Basic Skills Action Plan of each Lifelong Learning Partnership;
- advising each Partnership on their Action Plan;
- promoting and disseminating good practice;
- coordinating and promoting the professional development of teachers;
- promoting basic skills nationally;
- assessing progress against targets.

12.7 Much support will be needed as back-up for these functions, and we recommend that the Basic Skills Agency be asked to provide this, building on its present activities. Independence will help to achieve the involvement that is needed nationally and locally. The National Strategy focuses on Partnerships between a range of local organisations and groups, the individuals in need and the Government that serves them. The independence of the Agency, a body close to Government, will help to ensure coherence and credibility. The Minister of State for Education and Employment, Baroness Blackstone said in a recent talk given to the Agency's Board of Management:

'The Agency has an important independent and lobbying role and sometimes its messages may be critical and at times even uncomfortable for Government; but it has a crucial role to play in raising standards'.

12.8 We recognise that these responsibilities would necessitate some changes in the structure and operation of the Agency. The Board of Management of the Agency, in collaboration with the DfEE, would need to consider these potential changes in relation to the implementation of the National Strategy.

12.9 While the inspection of basic skills programmes would continue to be undertaken by the inspection organisations, the Basic Skills Agency should monitor the progress of the Action Plans, and report on progress as part of its existing role in reporting to the Secretary of State annually about basic skills provision.

12.10 Within Government, as is clear, the lead responsibility falls to the Department for Education and Employment. But many other government departments must play a part in reaching and teaching adults with basic skills needs. For example:

- the Home Office should continue its crucial work in meeting basic skills needs within the prison population; and should also require probation services to extend the scope and effectiveness of their basic skills programmes;
- the Ministry of Defence should ensure that no member of the Armed Services, who enlists with poor basic skills, is left unable to cope with the literacy and numeracy demands of service life;
- the Department of Health, building on its commitment to education as a plank of long-term health gain, must look to new ways to make basic skills gain a part of Healthy Living Centres, Health Action Zones, and a part of the primary health care strategies of its providers;
- the DTI should find ways to ensure that basic skills finds its way into the competitiveness agenda of its agencies and of companies in general;
- the Department for the Environment, Transport and the Regions, through its housing, regeneration and other programmes, can reach large numbers of adults with basic skills needs and provide effective support in basic skills that will improve the capacity and enhance the life opportunities of many;
- and the Social Exclusion Unit should take account of the evidence on the impact of poor basic skills on individuals, their reduced opportunities and their potential exclusion from society.

12.11 In short, many government departments can contribute to the achievement of our goals, recognising the potential benefits of improved basic skills in their respective spheres. One cannot stress too often that poor basic skills can affect individuals in many aspects of life, calling for joint commitment, joint planning and joint action to make a concerted difference to their lives.

RECOMMENDATION 18 – A National Strategy Group

A new National Adult Basic Skills Strategy Group, with Ministerial chairmanship, should be established by the Secretary of State to oversee the implementation of the National Strategy. It should be supported by a Technical Implementation Sub-Committee.

RECOMMENDATION 19 – Role of the Basic Skills Agency

The role and responsibility of the Basic Skills Agency should be revised so that, building on its present responsibilities, it can:

(i) advise each Partnership on their Action Plan;

(ii) promote and disseminate good practice;

(iii) coordinate and promote the professional development of teachers;

(iv) promote basic skills nationally;

(v) assess progress against targets;

(vi) report to the Secretary of State each year on progress towards meeting the national target.

Chapter 13: Funding

13.1 The National Strategy proposed in this Report envisages activities at many levels, national, regional and local. Public and private bodies are involved, and for everyone some spending may be required. What precisely will be needed depends entirely on the scale and timing of implementation.

Present costs

13.2 The starting point must be present costs. In fact it is difficult to get precise information about current expenditure on all activities concerned with provision for adults. This is largely because most funding does not separate basic skills from other education and training. For example, though information about FEFC funding of Programme Area 10 is available, it covers more than literacy and numeracy provision. Similarly, while information is available about additional support for students in colleges, often this is wider than support for basic skills.

13.3 The Local Government Association is not able to identify the amount spent by LEAs on basic skills provision for adults, which are another important source of funding. There are similar problems in disaggregating relevant funding from other sources, such as TECs, the Single Regeneration Budget, the Lottery, Trusts and Foundations and the European Union. So any estimate of current expenditure is approximate.

13.4 The absence of detailed information about funding emphasises the case we make for consistency and coherence. These are essential for the funding arrangements in the new National Strategy and for Local Action Plans. To ensure consistency and coherence, we propose that there should be a single funding mechanism in the future.

13.5 We turn to the additional funding necessary to achieve the targets in the National Strategy. Our estimates are bound to be approximate, largely because of uncertainty about total current expenditure. Also, depending on which of our key recommendations are implemented, there should be greater efficiency in future arrangements. So the figures below are somewhat speculative, and will need to be refined by the proposed Technical Implementation Group. This is vital, not just because our estimates are approximate, but also because many of the recommendations raise policy issues dependent more on principles than on costs. Once they are approved in principle, timing and costs can be realistically assessed.

13.6 At present (1997/8) some £280 million a year is spent in England on basic skills for people over 19, of which £180 million is spent by the Further Education Funding Council (FEFC). Table 13.1 sets out the details. The FEFC funds approximately 250,000 learners at a cost of £750 per learner. Each learner is studying on average for about 1.6 qualifications – for example one in literacy and one in numeracy. The present success rate is low, with about one third of learners achieving their learning goal.[54]

Table 13.1: Expenditure on basic skills programmes by source of funding 1997/98

Source of Funding	£m
FEFC funding (including Summer Schools)	180
Prisons	23
Family Literacy	4
Adult and Community Learning Fund	3
European Social Fund	27
Other Government Initiatives (planned)	7
National Lottery	32
TOTAL	**£ 276**

Future learner numbers and costs

13.7 Against this background, a rough estimate of future costs can be made.

13.8 The Government has committed itself to a large expansion in basic skills provision between 1997/98 and 2001/02. The target is to double the number of learners from 250,000 per year to 500,000, and it is a fair expectation that FEFC expenditure may also double from £180 million to over £350 million by 2001/02.

13.9 To achieve the targets for improving literacy and numeracy proposed here will require further expansion thereafter. The aim is to reduce the numbers with inadequate literacy by 3,500,000 by the year 2010, with a similar target for numeracy. This means that on average each year some 450,000 people will have to achieve functional literacy and a similar number functional numeracy. The aim for 2005 must be that 450,000 people are achieving this.

13.10 This is a formidable challenge. At present the comparable flow of successful learners is under 70,000 per annum. The flow of successful learners has therefore to increase by more than sixfold. At the present rate of success and cost, the total cost of achieving the targets would also have to be six times as high as at present – over £1,100 million.

13.11 This would be an unrealistic aim financially, and we propose a more radical approach. Our proposals are focused on a much more efficient system, in which the failure rate among learners on programmes is drastically cut (from its present level of two-thirds) and some learners are able to raise their standards largely by independent learning, often through the University for Industry. We believe that our targets can be achieved by a well-organised system in which the number of funded learners rises from 500,000 in 2001/02 to 750,000 in 2005/06, remaining level thereafter.

13.12 How much would this cost? Clearly we are envisaging a much higher average quality of provision per learner than at present. On the other hand, a larger and better organised system offers significant economies of scale. To assess the balance of these effects should be an early task for the Implementation Group. The factors to take into account include the following:

(i) current FEFC provision envisages that learners will typically receive 70 hours of guided learning per qualification. If the success rate is to be improved, the average number of hours will have to be increased substantially;

(ii) on the other hand, for certain types of course, especially those relying on the University for Industry, the cost per learner hour can be reduced substantially.

13.13 Our provisional calculations suggest that there will have to be some increase in the expenditure per funded learner if our targets for outcomes are to be achieved. At the very least we envisage that, whilst at present the average learner is taking 1.6 qualifications, in future equal numbers would be tackling literacy and numeracy.[55] If we allow only for that, the calculation for the year 2005/06 is simple. Starting from £180 million in 1997/98, we would treble it for the increase in student numbers and add another 25% for the increased number of qualifications studied for. This leads to around £680 million. On this basis the cost would rise steadily by £60-£65 million a year, from £180 million in 1997/98 to £350 million in 2000/01 and £680 million in 2005/06, remaining constant thereafter. It is a very preliminary estimate and the Implementation Group will need to refine it.

13.14 A broad picture emerges as follows. At present, the main cost from FEFC funding is £180 million per annum. It is a fair assumption that, to achieve the expansion in numbers which is already official policy, the figure for 2000/01 will be of the order of £350 million. The full implementation of the National Strategy proposed here would raise this to some £680 million by 2005/06, five years later.

Other costs

13.15 There is no doubt that by far the largest cost implication of the proposed National Strategy is that discussed above, i.e. the effect of increasing student numbers. Some of the other recommendations are cost-neutral, and for yet others – for example, promotion campaigns by broadcasters and the media – the costs will not directly involve public expenditure. For quite a few items, re-focusing of an institution's existing funding would be the required course.

13.16 Amongst the other recommendations which will clearly have additional public expenditure implications, we would single out:

- training of teachers
- the workplace-based Basic Skills Development Fund
- day-release arrangements
- expansion of family literacy and numeracy programmes
- development of the core curriculum and support materials.

13.17 All these rest on policy decisions dependent on matters of principle rather than on costs. Once these decisions of principle have been made, costs and timing estimates can follow. This is a task the Technical Implementation Sub-Committee would need to undertake. But, at this stage, our rough estimate is that the recommendations requiring additional costs outlined in the Implementation Plan, if fully implemented, might add some £30 million to the annual cost. It is our hope that a number of the key initiatives, with quite modest costs, will be put in train by the Ministerial Group, so progress is made towards the targets even before the precise long-term targets and their costs are established.

13.18 There are some interim measures to consider. Deciding on the allocation of resources and changing funding mechanisms inevitably takes time, and it is important to make progress with the broad thrust of the National Strategy meanwhile. An urgent task is for the Further Education Funding Council, TECs and other major funding bodies to modify their funding mechanisms so as to provide an incentive for providers to increase the scale of what they offer. In addition, the FEFC should increase the entry units for basic skills to encourage the outreach work that is essential if more learners are to be brought into programmes.

13.19 We also propose that the FEFC, TEC and other funding bodies should give priority to funding more intensive courses of at least 10 hours a week.

RECOMMENDATION 20 – Funding

(i) A priority for the Technical Implementation Sub-Committee should be to produce more definitive estimates of all the costs involved in the National Strategy, refining the broad estimates made here.

(ii) The FEFC, TECs and other major funding bodies should modify their funding mechanisms to provide incentives for providers to increase the scale of adult basic skills provision.

(iii) The FEFC should increase the entry units for basic skills to encourage outreach work, and to account for the requirement of institutions to assess all appropriate students.

Chapter 14: Further Research and Development

14.1 Despite much work in recent years, research about basic skills difficulties amongst adults is sparse. General information exists about the scale of the problem – although information about different levels and types of need is more difficult to come by – and the impact of poor basic skills has been well documented. The work of Professor John Bynner and his colleagues, now at the Centre for Longitudinal Studies at the Institute for Education (University of London), and research stemming from the International Adult Literacy Survey, are foremost among these. Within the next year, a research project conducted by the National Foundation for Educational Research for the Basic Skills Agency will throw light on the effectiveness of programmes.

14.2 However, there are major knowledge gaps, some of which have hampered our work. Little has been done to estimate the benefits gained from skills improvements, by individuals let alone the economy as a whole. Nor is much information available about whether improved basic skills are sustained and further developed over time. Too little is known about the relative cost effectiveness of different approaches.

14.3 The most complete evidence available to us related to the scale of need. It is particularly important to keep up research and survey work to gather such information, and to use it to inform the development of the National Strategy.

14.4 We propose that the Government should commission a baseline scale of need survey. The existing IALS survey is not entirely suitable for this purpose, since it does not deal effectively with numeracy skills, and does not allow one to differentiate between those with very low and low literacy skills. Any new survey should give greater emphasis to identifying low levels of skill, and should be the baseline from which the Technical Implementation Sub-Committee would set specific, realistic and demanding yet achievable targets for the future. However the survey should be formulated in such a way as to allow the results to be linked into the main international surveys, since it is vital that we are able to compare our progress against that of other countries.

14.5 There must be continued use of longitudinal studies, including the NCDS study that we have drawn on in this report. In this context, the work of Professor Bynner and his colleagues is particularly important. These studies provide the most effective information, based on a large number of adults, on levels of need and the impact of poor basic skills. We should ensure that future cohort sweeps continue to gather data on categories and types of need, and how they are changing in the light of new measures. In particular, questioning should be directed at issues such as:

- benefits obtained from improving basic skills and gaining qualifications later in adult life;
- basic skills components of social exclusion, including unemployment, health problems and crime and the means by which individuals and groups are able to overcome them;
- inter-generational continuities and discontinuities in basic skills and what affects them.

14.6 We recommend continued participation in the OECD International Adult Literacy Survey. Although reservations have been expressed about the size of the sample and some technical aspects, it provides the best comparative information about how we as a nation measure up alongside European and other international countries. We note that IALS is now being revised.

14.7 Past research has focused on problems with reading and to a lesser extent with numberwork, using specially designed tests to assess the extent of an individual's problems. Future work is required on such issues as:

- literacy and numeracy problems for second language speakers;
- writing difficulties and proficiency at all levels;
- oral communication skills;
- IT literacy and further extension to other key skills;
- relationships between literacy and numeracy and special learning difficulties.

14.8 Perhaps one reason why no country has yet discovered ready solutions for poor literacy, numeracy and language fluency is because there is little evidence of what teaching methods and assessment methods work best with adults who have problems. We propose that the DfEE and the Basic Skills Agency explore the potential for an international research project into this issue.

14.9 There are other research areas meriting attention in relation to basic skills issues. We would note in particular:

- research on special needs, including particularly issues for adults with dyslexia;
- research on assessment procedures;
- research on higher level literacy and numeracy needs in particular occupations.

14.10 We would also welcome an international study of how basic skills are tackled in various countries, and how well policies and initiatives work.

Evaluation of the strategy

14.11 There should be a regular evaluation of the National Strategy, and especially of:

- the operation of local Partnerships, and their effectiveness in setting and reaching targets for improvement in the adult population;
- the effectiveness of promotion campaigns, and the numbers of adults joining and staying in programmes;
- the promotion, use, take-up and acquisition of new qualifications;
- progress in achieving participation in programmes, and consequent improvements in basic skills;
- the working of the various assessment arrangements.

14.12 The timescale for this research must mirror the timescale for the development and implementation of the National Strategy itself. Meanwhile, the first phase of research into the effectiveness of programmes should be completed by September 2000, so that partnerships can then use this information to develop their Action Plans.

RECOMMENDATION 21 – Research

The Department for Education and Employment should ensure that a research programme is set up to provide a systematic basis for the proposed strategy, including continuous monitoring of Action Plans. This should be done in collaboration with the Basic Skills Agency.

Recommendations

Chapter 5 – A National Strategy and a National Target

RECOMMENDATION 1 – A National Basic Skills Strategy for Adults

The Government should launch a National Strategy to reduce the number of adults with low levels of basic skills.

RECOMMENDATION 2 – National Targets

(i) As part of the National Strategy, the Government should commit itself to the virtual elimination of functional illiteracy and innumeracy.

(ii) In addition to the accepted participation target for 2002, the Government should set specific basic skills targets for adults and for young people to be achieved by 2005 and 2010, on the scale proposed in the new National Strategy.

Chapter 6 – Increasing Participation

RECOMMENDATION 3 – A National Campaign

There should be a continuous high profile promotion campaign, with clear segmentation for different groups of learners, to be devised by a new Adult Basic Skills Promotion Task Force. This should be set up in 2000.

Chapter 7 – Entitlement

RECOMMENDATION 4 – Entitlement

(i) All adults with basic skills below Level 2 should be entitled to a confidential assessment of their skills on demand, access to high quality information, advice and guidance, and access to a variety of programmes of study – all free of charge.

(ii) People who have successfully completed basic skills courses should be a priority target for the first million Individual Learning Accounts funded from TEC resources to help them progress.

(iii) The Government should consider how, in the long term, Individual Learning Accounts can be most effectively used to motivate these learners.

Chapter 8 – Expanding and Improving Opportunities

RECOMMENDATION 5 – Programmes for the Unemployed

(i) The Government should:

a) ensure that the basic skills of all New Deal clients are assessed soon after they make contact with their Personal Adviser, and that intensive basic skills courses are offered early on to those with basic skills at Entry Level or below;

b) ensure that all claimants for benefit are entitled to assessment of basic skills and offered effective provision to improve their skills if below Level 2.

(ii) The New Deal Task Force should be asked urgently to ensure that clients with basic skills below Level 2, on options other than the education and training option, get access to basic skills support.

(iii) Training should be provided for all Personal Advisers so that they can identify basic skills needs and encourage the take-up of basic skills opportunities where this is necessary.

RECOMMENDATION 6 – Workplace Programmes

(i) The Government should set up a Workplace Basic Skills Development Fund. This would provide seed funding for companies to set up basic skills programmes either in the workplace or at a local institution such as a college or adult education centre.

(ii) Up to a fixed budget limit, the Government should finance the wage cost of day release for up to 13 weeks for people with basic skills below Level 1.

(iii) The revised *Investors in People* guidance should include a requirement for companies to have effective arrangements for assessing and dealing with basic skills difficulties.

(iv) Training for basic skills at the workplace should be funded on a par with funding of such programmes in FE Colleges.

(v) A 'pledge' scheme for companies should be introduced to allow them to indicate their support for raising standards of basic skills among adults.

RECOMMENDATION 7 – Trade Unions

(i) Unions should provide basic skills programmes for their members based on the new National Strategy.

(ii) Unions should work with the TUC to train and develop "union learning representatives", who should support and advise learners and work with employers on the development of basic skills provision in the workplace.

(iii) Unions should be encouraged to submit bids to the Union Learning Fund, and the Workplace Basic Skills Development Fund, for the development of basic skills programmes.

RECOMMENDATION 8 – The University for Industry

In pursuing its commitment to making basic skills a priority, the UfI should:

(a) ensure that learners undertaking courses below Level 2 through UfI-endorsed programmes should have access to, and guidance on, basic skills help available;

(b) ensure that in working towards its targets for basic skills support in the workplace and elsewhere, materials, tutor support and qualifications meet the quality standards we propose;

(c) commission multimedia basic skills products, on-line learning and digital TV programmes, to provide for adults with basic skills needs through learning centres and at home.

RECOMMENDATION 9 – Community Based Programmes

Local Basic Skills Action Plans should specifically include community based provision to meet increased local need, for which particular resources should be identified. The Secretary of State should take account of the adequacy of such community-based provision in approving local Adult Basic Skills Action Plans.

RECOMMENDATION 10 – Basic Skills Support in Colleges

(i) As soon as possible, and no later than 2002, all providers funded by FEFC should, as a requirement of funding, be required to assess all appropriate students enrolling and offer additional support.

(ii) By 2002 all students assessed as requiring additional support with basic skills in colleges should be able to take up this help.

RECOMMENDATION 11 – Family-Based Programmes

(i) All infant and primary schools in educationally disadvantaged areas should have family literacy and numeracy programmes by 2002.

(ii) the Basic Skills Agency should continue to develop and evaluate new models of family literacy and family numeracy programmes.

Chapter 9 – Quality

RECOMMENDATION 12 – Quality Assurance

By 2002 all basic skills programmes should be required to meet a new nationally determined framework of standards in order to qualify for funding.

RECOMMENDATION 13 – Inspection

The three inspection agencies, FEFC, OFSTED and TSC, should work together on a common inspection framework based on clear and transparent standards and consistent with the proposed national quality framework.

RECOMMENDATION 14 – Teacher Training

(i) All new staff and volunteers should undertake recognised initial training in teaching literacy and numeracy to adults.

(ii) The BSA and the new Further Education National Training Organisation (FENTO) and others should work together to produce new qualifications for teaching basic skills to adults.

(iii) By 2005 all teachers of basic skills should have this qualification or an equivalent.

(iv) Diploma courses in teaching basic skills to adults should be established in University Education Departments.

(v) Intensive courses for teachers to become familiar with the new curriculum should be mounted.

RECOMMENDATION 15 – Use of Information and Communication Technology

In view of the importance of Information and Communication Technology in basic skills learning programmes, the DfEE should ensure, in collaboration with relevant bodies, that such programmes receive all the necessary advice and support.

Chapter 10 – Core Curriculum and Qualifications

RECOMMENDATION 16 – Core Curriculum and Qualifications

(i) There should be a new national basic skills curriculum for adults, with well-defined standards of skill at Entry Level, Level 1 and Level 2.

(ii) Only basic skills qualifications based on this new curriculum should be funded from the public purse. Whether assessed by coursework, test or a mixture of both they should use a common set of standards laid down by QCA.

(iii) Existing qualifications should be revised to meet these new national standards.

(iv) Existing qualifications based exclusively on tests should be replaced by a new National Literacy Test and a new National Numeracy Test both available at Levels 1 and 2.

Chapter 11 – Delivery of the Strategy

RECOMMENDATION 17 – Local Partnerships

(i) Implementing the National Strategy locally should be the responsibility of the local Lifelong Learning Partnerships. These would include representatives of those concerned with adult basic skills. Their composition would be submitted to the Secretary of State for guidance.

(ii) Each Partnership should be required to submit an Action Plan for the approval of the Secretary of State.

Chapter 12 – National Coordination

RECOMMENDATION 18 – A National Strategy Group

A new National Adult Basic Skills Strategy Group, with Ministerial chairmanship, should be established by the Secretary of State to oversee the implementation of the National Strategy. It should be supported by a Technical Implementation Sub-Committee.

RECOMMENDATION 19 – Role of the Basic Skills Agency

The role and responsibility of the Basic Skills Agency should be revised so that, building on its present responsibilities, it can:

(i) advise each Partnership on their Action Plan;

(ii) promote and disseminate good practice;

(iii) coordinate and promote the professional development of teachers;

(iv) promote basic skills nationally;

(v) assess progress against targets;

(vi) report to the Secretary of State each year on progress towards meeting the national target.

Chapter 13 – Funding

RECOMMENDATION 20 – Funding

(i) A priority for the Technical Implementation Sub-Committee should be to produce more definitive estimates of all the costs involved in the National Strategy, refining the broad estimates made here.

(ii) The FEFC, TECs and other major funding bodies should modify their funding mechanisms to provide incentives for providers to increase the scale of adult basic skills provision.

(iii) The FEFC should increase the entry units for basic skills to encourage outreach work, and to account for the requirement of institutions to assess all appropriate students.

Chapter 14 – Further Research and Development

RECOMMENDATION 21 – Research

The Department for Education and Employment should ensure that a research programme is set up to provide a systematic basis for the proposed strategy, including continuous monitoring of Action Plans. This should be done in collaboration with the Basic Skills Agency.

Implementation Plan

Recommendation	Date to be achieved	Responsibility	Identifiable additional costs
1 A National Strategy Adoption of the National Strategy	April 1999	DfEE	–
2 A National Target Setting of National Targets	September 1999	National Adult Basic Skills Strategy Group	The costs of the proposed targets are discussed in Chapter 13
3 Increasing Participation Establishment of Promotion Task Group	2000	UfI/BBC/BSA	–
Launch of high profile promotion campaign	2000	National Adult Basic Skills Strategy Group	£5 million from DfEE Additional contributions from media companies
4 Entitlement Entitlement for all adults with basic skills below Level 2 to: a confidential assessment of their skills on demand; access to high quality information, advice and guidance; access to a variety of programmes of study – all free of charge	September 2000	DfEE	–
Adults who have successfully completed basic skills courses should be a priority target for the first million Individual Learning Accounts funded from TEC resources	January 2000	DfEE/TECs	–
The Government should consider how, in the long term, Individual Learning Accounts can be most effectively used to motivate these learners	2000	DfEE	–
5 Programmes for the Unemployed All New Deal clients to be assessed for basic skills difficulties soon after making contact with their Personal Adviser	September 1999	Employment Service	–
Intensive basic skills courses available at early stage for New Dealers with basic skills at Entry Level or below	September 1999	Employment Service/Providers	–

Recommendation	Date to be achieved	Responsibility	Identifiable additional costs
All claimants for benefit entitled to assessment of basic skills and offered effective provision to improve their skills	January 2002	Benefits Agency	–
New Deal Task Force to ensure that clients with basic skills below Level 2 on options other than the education and training option get access to basic skills support	September 1999	New Deal Task Force	–
Training for Personal Advisers in identifying basic skills so that they can identify basic skills needs and encourage the take-up of basic skills opportunities	Begin May 1999	Employment Service/BSA	–
6 Workplace Programmes Establishment of Workplace Basic Skills Development Fund	April 2000	DfEE	Size of Fund to be determined by the DfEE
Up to a fixed budget limit, funding available for the wage cost of day release for up to 13 weeks for people with basic skills below Level 1	July 2001	DfEE	Scale of funding to be decided by the DfEE
Requirement to have effective arrangements for diagnosing and handling basic skills difficulties included in Investors in People guidance	September 2000	IiP UK	–
Funding available for basic skills training in the workplace on a par with funding in FE Colleges	September 2000	DfEE/FEFC	–
'Pledge' scheme for major companies launched	September 1999	DfEE	–
7 Trade Unions TUC promote significant role for trade unions in basic skills, including: • unions providing basic skills programmes • training and developing "union learning representatives"	Begin May 1999	TUC/BSA	–

Recommendation	Date to be achieved	Responsibility	Identifiable additional costs
Unions encouraged to submit bids to the Union Learning Fund and the Workplace Basic Skills Development Fund for the development of basic skills programmes	September 1999	DfEE/TUC/BSA	–
8 The University for Industry All learners on UfI-endorsed courses with basic skills below Level 2 should have access to, and guidance on, basic skills help available	September 2000	UfI	To depend on overall UfI budget
Commission of multimedia basic skills products, development of on-line learning and digital TV provision	January 2000	UfI	To depend on overall UfI budget
UfI materials, tutor support and qualifications meet new national quality standards	January 2000	UfI/DfEE/BSA	–
9 Community Based Programmes Local Basic Skills Action Plans to include adequate community based provision to meet local need	December 1999	Lifelong Learning Partnerships/DfEE/BSA	–
10 Basic Skills Support Initial and diagnostic assessment, and offer of additional support for those below Level 2, a requirement of funding for all FEFC and TEC funded programmes	January 2002	DfEE/FEFC/TECs	–
11 Family Based Programmes Establishment of family literacy and numeracy programmes in infant and primary schools in areas of highest need	September 2000	DfEE/SEU	£17.5 million*
Basic Skills Agency to develop and evaluate new models of family literacy and family numeracy programmes	Begin May 1999	BSA	–
12 Quality Assurance All basic skills programmes required to meet a new nationally determined framework of standards to qualify for funding.	September 2001	DfEE/Lifelong Learning Partnerships/BSA/TECs	£200,000 development costs

**Based on current Standards Fund funding of £3,500 per course, for 5,000 primary schools (25% of all schools) = £17.5 million*

Recommendation	Date to be achieved	Responsibility	Identifiable additional costs
13 Inspection			
FEFC, OFSTED and TSC to develop a common inspection framework with rigorous, clear and transparent standards based on the proposed national quality framework.	December 1999	DfEE/Inspection Agencies	–
14 Teacher Training			
All new staff and volunteers required to undertake initial training in teaching literacy and numeracy to adults	September 1999	DfEE/FEFC/TECs/ BSA	–
Development of new qualifications for teaching basic skills to adults	Begin April 1999	QCA/BSA/ FENTO	£250,000
Diploma courses in teaching basic skills to adults established in University Education Departments	September 2001	FENTO	–
All teachers of basic skills required to hold the new qualification or an equivalent	2005	DfEE/FEFC/TECs/ BSA	–
Intensive courses on teaching to the new curriculum for existing teachers	Begin September 1999	DfEE/BSA/ FENTO	£1.5 million*
15 Use of Information and Communication Technology			
Basic skills programmes receive advice and support to ensure that ICT is used effectively for teaching adult basic skills	January 2000	DfEE	£200,000 (for research, publication and dissemination; additional cost of providing hardware to be determined in the light of future policy decisions)
16 Core Curriculum and Qualifications			
Development of a new basic skills core curriculum for adults	September 1999	BSA/QCA/SEU	£900,000 (for development and publication of curriculum document and teaching materials /support)

**Based on 1,000 full-time staff + 4,000 part-time staff x 1 days training x £300 staffing and development = £1.5 million*

Recommendation	Date to be achieved	Responsibility	Identifiable additional costs
All publicly funded programmes to use the new basic skills core curriculum for adults	January 2000	DfEE/FEFC/TECs/ BSA	–
All publicly funded basic skills qualifications to be based on this curriculum and rigorous standards	January 2001	QCA/FEFC/TECs/ BSA	–
New National Literacy Test and National Numeracy Test introduced at Levels 1 and 2	January 2001	QCA	–
17 Delivery of the Strategy Lifelong Learning Partnerships required to submit three-year Basic Skills Action Plans to Secretary of State	December 1999	Lifelong Learning Partnerships/BSA	–
18 National Coordination Establishment of a National Adult Basic Skills Strategy Group and a Technical Implementation Sub-Committee to oversee implementation of National Strategy	April 1999	DfEE	–
19 Role of the Basic Skills Agency Basic Skills Agency to undertake independent support role including advice to Partnerships and Secretary of State, dissemination of good practice, assessing progress against targets	Ongoing from April 1999	BSA/DfEE	£1.5 million (estimate of funding required to increase the capacity of the Agency to meet recommendations)
20 Funding Additional resources allocated for the National Basic Skills Strategy	April 2002	DfEE	Additional resources for the strategy are discussed in full in Chapter 13
Major funders modify funding mechanisms to encourage increase in the scale of basic skills provision	April 2000	DfEE/FEFC/TECs	–
FEFC increase entry units for basic skills to encourage outreach	April 2000	FEFC	–
21 Research Establishment of research programme to support the strategy	Ongoing from May 1999	National Adult Basic Skills Strategy Group	

Notes

1 See *It Doesn't Get Any Better,* Bynner and Parsons, The Basic Skills Agency, 1997 and *Adult Literacy in Britain,* Office for National Statistics, 1997 which give figures of 19% and 22% respectively.

2 *It Doesn't Get Any Better,* Bynner and Parsons, The Basic Skills Agency, 1997.

3 *Lost Opportunities,* Carr-Hill, Passingham, Wolf & Kent, The Basic Skills Agency, 1995.

4 *A Nation's Neglect,* The Basic Skills Agency, 1989.

5 'Trends in standards of literacy in the United Kingdom, 1948-1996', *Paper presented at UK Reading Association Conference, September 1997,* Dr Greg Brooks, NFER.

6 'Change in the reading attainment of adults: a longitudinal study', Rodgers, *British Journal of Developmental Psychology, 4 1-17,* 1986.

7 *Literacy Skills for the Knowledge Society,* Human Resource Development Canada/Organisation for Economic Cooperation and Development, 1997.

8 *Use It or Lose It?,* Bynner and Parsons, The Basic Skills Agency, 1998.

9 *The Basic Skills of Young Adults,* Ekinsmyth and Bynner, The Basic Skills Agency, 1994.

10 *Inclusive Learning: Report of the Learning Difficulties and/or Disabilities Committee,* FEFC, 1996.

11 The correlation of annual earnings with literacy is 0.28 and with numeracy 0.38. Source: International Adult Literacy Survey special analysis.

12 *The relative importance of education and ability for earnings: a speculative assessment,* C. Dougherty, London School of Economics, 1997.

13 *Schooling, Labour Force Quality, and the Growth of Nations,* E.A. Hanushek and D. Kim, National Bureau of Economic Research (USA), 1996.

14 Literacy is prose literacy and numeracy is quantitative literacy. Low level of literacy and numeracy is defined as IALS Level 1: high level of literacy and numeracy is defined as IALS Levels 4 and 5.

15 *Does Numeracy Matter?,* Bynner and Parsons, The Basic Skills Agency, 1997.

16 *Parents and their Children, ALBSU, 1993.*

17 This is bourne out in *Influences on Adults Basic Skills,* Parsons and Bynner, The Basic Skills Agency, 1998.

18 *Literacy Skills for the Knowledge Society,* HRDC/OECD, 1997.

19 *Bringing Britain together; a national strategy for neighbourhood renewal,* Report by the Social Exclusion Unit, 1998.

20 *Influences on Adult Basic Skills,* Bynner and Parsons, The Basic Skills Agency, 1998.

21 *Basic Skills and Jobs,* Institute for Employment Studies/ALBSU, 1993.

22 *ibid.*

23 This survey, by Gallup for ALBSU, involved 400 companies in England and Wales and was representative of employment sectors in the UK. *[The Cost to British Industry: Basic Skills and the Workforce, ALBSU 1993].*

24 *It Doesn't Get Any Better,* Bynner and Parsons, The Basic Skills Agency, 1997.

25 *Staying the Course,* The Basic Skills Agency, 1997.

26 *Staying the Course,* The Basic Skills Agency, 1997.

27 *Basic Education: Curriculum Area Survey Report,* FEFC, April 1998.

28 For example, over the years 1985-86 to 1991-92 learners in basic skills programmes in California made, on average, about 3-5 point improvement in 100 hours of instruction. This is about 0.5 a year in terms of improvement in Reading Age. Based on these results it is estimated that the average learner would require about 660 hours of instruction to get to a functional literacy level. Most basic skills courses in England provide between 80-150 hours of instruction in a year.

29 *Effective Basic Skills Provision for Adults,* The Basic Skills Agency, 1999.

30 It was estimated in 1987 that about 8% of adults with basic skills problems had 'learning difficulties'. *[Literacy, Numeracy and Adults, ALBSU 1987].*

31 *Time to Leave? Progression and Drop Out in Basic Skills Programmes,* Institute of Education/The Basic Skills Agency, 1994.

32 *On the Move: The BBC's contribution to the Adult Literacy Campaign in the UK between 1972 and 1976,* Hargreaves, 1980.

33 North West Basic Skills Helpline Promotions Campaign Research Project, IRB, 1997.

34 The Read and Write Together campaign aimed to motivate parents with poor basic skills to get help to improve their own basic skills in order to help their children. Parents were encouraged to call for a free pack which would give them ideas about activities to carry out with their children to develop their child's literacy skills.

35 The campaign won the BT award for TV marketing.

36 ABC Canada is a Canadian national non-profit literacy organisation, working in partnership with the media, business, labour, educators and government. The organisation focuses on continuous public awareness

programmes aimed at bringing more adults into basic skills learning.

37 A study by Bury CVS found that over 60% of local agency referred students left within 3 months, whilst over half of those who were self referred stayed for more than a year. *[Special Development Projects Report, 1978].*

38 See, for example, *Cornwall Adult Basic Education Service: Access to Adult Learning in a Rural Area,* OFSTED, 1998; *Developments in Basic Education: Special Development Projects 1978-85,* Charnley and Withnall, 1989, *North Essex Adult Community College Development Support Final Report,* Basic Skills Agency, 1997, *Tamworth and Lichfield Colleges.*

39 *Adult Literacy in the United States: a compendium of quantitative data and interpretive comments,* Sticht and Armstrong, 1994.

40 Local Needs Surveys England Cumulative data, ORB, 1997.

41 *Use It or Lose It?,* Bynner and Parsons, The Basic Skills Agency, 1998.

42 *Towards a National Skills Agenda,* National Skills Task Force, DfEE, 1998.

43 By appropriate we mean all students, except those where:

- the level of basic skills can be assumed – such as those on basic skills courses or with significant learning difficulties;
- those on higher education courses;
- those where the entry qualifications for the course would act as a proxy for good basic skills;
- those enrolling in non-vocational, part-time adult education courses.

44 Including targets for the percentage of need served by a programme, retention, progress and positive outcomes.

45 For good examples see *Cornwall Adult Education Service: Access to Adult Learning in a Rural Area,* OFSTED, 1998; *Shropshire STOP Project: something can be done,* Be Consultancy, 1998; *Step to Health Local Development Project Final Report,* The Basic Skills Agency, 1996.

46 See *London Connection Local Development Project,* ALBSU, 1995.

47 By *appropriate* we mean:

- a ratio of one paid teacher or trainer to a maximum of 6-8 learners where the majority of the learners are at a very basic level;
- a ratio of one paid teacher or trainer to a maximum of 8-12 learners where the majority of the learners are at an intermediate level.

48 *Literacy Learning through Technology,* Adult Literacy National Project, 1998

49 For example *LiteracyLink,* a partnership between government, educators and broadcasters to create online services for adult learners and educators to enable adult learners to use technology (including television) to improve basic skills. [See www.Pbs.org/insidepbs/news/literacylink/html].

50 *Survey of Computer Hardware in FEFC Sector Colleges,* NCET, 1992.

51 The Basic Skills Agency has produced a CD ROM, *Adult Basic Skills,* which provides an estimate of the scale of need for literacy and numeracy in every local authority in England.

52 This local improvement target would have to relate to a national target adopted as part of the national strategy.

53 We would expect the range to include:

- 'dedicated' courses;
- basic skills support programmes;
- community based programmes, including programmes that link improvement of basic skills to economic and social regeneration of communities;
- family based programmes, such as family literacy and family numeracy;
- workplace programmes;
- programmes for the unemployed.

54 This includes all students who achieved their learning goal which may not include a qualification. *[Basic Education,* FEFC, 1998 (p.29)].

55 They may not all be the same students but our calculations can be performed as it they were – i.e. with 750,000 students all of whom take numeracy and literacy.

Annex A – Definitions of Poor Literacy and Poor Numeracy

1 Throughout the report we relate literacy and numeracy skills to three levels: Entry Level, Level 1 and Level 2. This annex aims to provide:

- an overview of the two main surveys on which our estimates of need are based;
- an outline of the competencies required for adults to reach each Level;
- the relationship between the Levels used in this report and alternative national levels;
- estimates of the scale of need;
- the definition of functional literacy and numeracy.

Surveys of need

2 The most recent surveys of the scale of need for literacy and numeracy skills in Britain are *Adult Literacy in Britain*[1], which forms part of the International Adult Literacy Survey (IALS), and the latest reports from the Centre for Longitudinal Studies at the Institute of Education[2], *It Doesn't Get any Better*[3] and *The Basic Skills of Young Adults*[4].

3 The British IALS survey is the first literacy survey to be carried out in Britain on a national random sample of adults of working age. The survey was undertaken by the Office for National Statistics in 1997, and covered a sample of 3,811 adults. The survey set assessment tasks taken from a range of contexts simulating the range of activities that adults would encounter in everyday life. The survey produced measurements for three broad categories of literacy. These are:

Prose literacy	Understanding and using information from text, e.g. understanding a newspaper article.
Document literacy	Locating and using information from other formats, e.g. reading a bus timetable
Quantitative literacy	Applying arithmetic operations to numbers embedded in print, e.g working out the price of a loan from an advert.

4 Each of the three scales measuring these dimensions of literacy were designed to range from 0 to 500, and were grouped into five literacy levels: Level 1 representing the lowest ability range and Level 5 the highest. Individuals were graded at one of 5 levels, from very low (level 1) to very high (level 5), depending on how they performed in the tasks. To be placed at a particular level respondents had to perform tasks at that level correctly and consistently. The definition of consistent performance was set at 80%.

5 The British results of IALS showed that around 22% of adults had very low literacy levels. The figures for quantitative literacy, a proxy for numeracy skills, showed that 23% of adults in Britain had very low skills.

6 The *Centre for Longitudinal Studies* has carried out a series of studies of adults' basic skills for the Basic Skills Agency. The findings come from two birth cohort studies. The first is the National Child Development Study (NCDS) which comprises a sample of over 17,000 people born in a single week in 1958. The other study, known as the 1970 British Cohort Study (BCS70), is similar in form, beginning with a sample of over 17,000 people born in a single week in 1970.

1 *Adult Literacy in Britain, Office for National Statistics, 1997*

2 *Previously based at the Social Statistics Research Unit, City University*

3 *It Doesn't Get any Better, Bynner and Parsons, The Basic Skills Agency 1997*

4 *The Basic Skills of Young Adults, Ekinsmyth and Bynner, The Basic Skills Agency 1994*

7 The most recent survey, It Doesn't Get Any Better, was carried out on a 10% sample of NCDS cohort members. It included a basic skills assessment, which comprised a set of functional literacy and numeracy tasks designed by the National Foundation for Educational Research (NFER). The tasks were grouped at different levels corresponding to the Basic Skills Agency (BSA) Basic Skills Standards. Each question was coded as correctly answered, incorrectly answered or not attempted, and these scores were grouped into four ability categories: "very low", "low", "average" and "good". The results were as follows:

8 Since the assessment tasks used in the NCDS survey were aligned to the BSA Standards, these figures provide an indication of performance that can be related to them. The survey found that people in the very low groups were generally below Entry Level in the skills they had acquired, and those in the low groups had skills at Entry Level, but were not fully competent at Level 1.

Table A1: Levels of literacy and numeracy among 37 year olds, based on CLS research

Skills Levels	Literacy%	Numeracy%
Very Low	6	23
Low	13	25
Average	38	25
Good	43	27

Source: *It Doesn't Get any Better*, 1997

Abridged basic skills standards

Writing Skills	Entry Level	Level 1	Level 2
Write accurate letters, notes, reports or messages	Write short simple notes or letters conveying up to two separate ideas	Write reports, letters or notes conveying up to four separate ideas	Write material in a specialised format (e.g formal letters, contracts, leaflets, CVs)
Complete forms or other pre-formatted documents	Fill in a basic form (e.g. write an order form, booking slip, receipt)	Complete a simple form (e.g. application form, time-sheet, claim form)	Complete an open-ended form requiring detailed information (e.g. accident report form, job application)
Write about ideas, feelings and experiences	Short, simple pieces up to two paragraphs	Personal writing in several paragraphs, e.g descriptions of people or places, letters	Write effectively to convey ideas, feelings and experiences in a variety of styles e.g. short stories, poems, newspaper articles

Reading Skills	**Entry Level**	**Level 1**	**Level 2**
Read and understand text in the form of letters, written instructions, manuals, notes, orders etc	Read and understand simple text (up to six sentences or one paragraph) Follow simple instructions (up to 6 steps, one per step)	Read and understand a variety of text (e.g a letter up to one page long, short features in a newspaper or magazine) Follow written instructions – each step could contain up to 3 short sentences	Choose and use appropriate materials from more than one source, e.g manuals, brochures, textbooks Understand the purpose and meaning in a text and make a judgement from the information
Read and understand graphical material such as tables, signs, charts, labels, plans, maps etc	Get the main idea from a simple source, (e.g safety signs with a single message) Find specific pieces of information from simple tables (no more than 2 variables)	Understand and act on a graphical source up to one page long (e.g. a town map, price list, sign with multiple messages) Find information from complex tables, with at least 2 variables and with additional sources/keys)	Select material from more than one graphical source (e.g complex tables, plans)
Use reference systems such as filing systems, libraries, databases	Use a simple list	Consult a reference source to obtain simple information (e.g. Yellow Pages, dictionary)	Use a reference system to find specific information e.g library, computer file, filing system Organise material into a given reference system – alphabetical, numerical or date order and use the system created

Numeracy Skills	**Entry Level**	**Level 1**	**Level 2**
Using money in everyday situations, using till, calculator or ready reckoner as necessary	Make cash or other transactions of up to seven similar items at a time, give or check correct change if necessary	Make cash and non-cash transactions of up to 20 items at a time, give or check correct change and calculate simple discounts. Share payments equally between 4-12 people	Make cash and non-cash transactions of any number of items at a time and calculate complex discounts from percentages and fractions. Check and give documentation, change and receipts. Share payments between a minimum of 4 people where costs are not shared equally
Calculate lengths, areas, weights or volumes accurately using appropriate tools, e.g. rulers, calculators etc	Simple calculations on familiar items in either metric or imperial units, e.g calculating areas of rectangles from lengths in the same whole unit	Calculations on items of unfamiliar or irregular shape in either metric or imperial units	Calculations on items of complex or composite shape, use scale drawings, convert between metric and imperial units
Make and monitor schedules or budgets in order to plan the use of time and money	Plan and monitor small amounts of time and money (up to 7 days or £250)	Plan and monitor amounts of time, money or expenditure (up to 4 weeks or £2000)	Plan and monitor large amounts of time money or spending (over 4 weeks or up to £20,000)
Keep records in numerical or graphical form	Record simple numerical information (e.g. count and report on small batches, quantities between 25 and 1000)	Find the appropriate information and make a simple record based on it (e.g simple stock taking) Extract, use, report or present information from/on tables, pie charts, bar charts, pictograms and line graphs Round numbers up or down and report the information orally or in writing	Find the appropriate information from several complex sources and make a record based on it. Choose appropriate tables and charts on which to present information including tables with more than 4 columns, a bar chart or pictogram (up to 3 variables, 4-8 reports), and line graphs

Oral Communication Skills	Entry Level	Level 1	Level 2
Give information to other people on the telephone or face to face	Give information on a single topic to one familiar person	Give information on several topics to unfamiliar people in a formal or semi-formal situation	Explain or describe things to people in order to help them Put and justify a case orally to one other person
Getting information from other people on the telephone or face to face	Getting information on a single topic from one familiar person	Getting information on several topics from unfamiliar people	Find, select and use appropriate information from several people to solve a problem

Relationship between different frameworks

9 It is also possible to relate the BSA Basic Skills Standards very approximately to the levels used in the QCA National Framework of Qualifications, and in the National Curriculum in schools. The NCDS results thus have the advantage of allowing us to make some broad estimates of how adults' basic skills needs fit into the national framework. This kind of mapping can never be perfect, but the broad equivalencies are as follows:

Table A2: Equivalent National Levels

BSA Standards	QCA National Framework of Qualifications	Equivalent Vocational Qualification	Equivalent Level in Schools
Entry	Entry	–	National Curriculum Level 2
Level 1	Foundation	Level 1 NVQ	National Curriculum Level 4
Level 2	Intermediate	Level 2 NVQ	GCSE grades A-C

10 It is not easy to establish equivalence between the IALS and NCDS surveys, since the two reports define basic skills in different ways, with different underlying conceptual frameworks and varying thresholds for defining competency. However, the Office for National Statistics suggest that tasks rated at Level 1 in IALS broadly relate to those rated at Entry Level, and some of the tasks rated at Level 1, of the BSA Standards.

Scale of need

11 The two surveys reach broadly similar conclusions about the scale of need for literacy, defined as 19% with poor literacy in the NCDS survey compared to 22% in IALS. There is, however, a discrepancy between the findings for the scale of need for numeracy – 48% in the NCDS survey compared to 23% in the IALS survey. We have chosen to use the NCDS figures as our guide for the approximate numbers of adults with numeracy difficulties, for the following reasons:

- the IALS research tested quantitative literacy skills, which is only a proxy for numeracy ability;

- since IALS was attempting to measure competence across the full ability range, very few tasks were used to distinguish those at the lower end of ability compared to the NCDS research;
- the IALS classification, due to its underlying statistical framework, tends to 'push' the sample into four similar quartiles, which may partly explain the similarity between the prose and quantitative literacy results.

12 Therefore, based on the survey evidence outlined above, our baseline throughout the report is that some 20% of adults have low literacy skills. We refer to these adults throughout the report as being "at Entry Level" or "below Level 1". Extrapolating from the rough mapping of equivalencies set out in Table A2, this means that these adults have not yet acquired the literacy skills required to achieve a Key Skills qualification in Communication at Level 1, or the skills required to be at Level 4 of the National Curriculum.

13 From the NCDS research we can estimate that roughly one third of the 20% (or 6% of all adults) have very low literacy. We refer to these adults as being "below Entry Level". Broadly, these adults do not have the literacy skills required to meet the standards set by a qualification such as Wordpower at Entry Level, or to carry out the Entry Level tasks set out in the basic skills standards table.

14 We can estimate from the NCDS research that as many as 48% of adults have low numeracy. As before, we refer to these adults as being "at Entry Level" or "below Level 1". As with literacy, a rough exercise suggests that these adults do not have adequate numeracy skills to achieve a Key Skills qualification in the application of number at Level 1.

15 Approximately half of these adults (or 23% of all adults) have very low numeracy. Throughout the report we refer to such adults as being "below Entry Level". As before, these adults will not have adequate numeracy skills to meet the standards of a qualification such as Numberpower at Entry level.

16 Our focus in the report is on the 1 in 5 adults with low literacy, and the 1 in 5 adults with very low numeracy. Since by far the majority of the adults in this group have difficulties with both literacy and numeracy, this corresponds to some 7 million adults in England.

Functional literacy and numeracy

17 This focus is based on our working definition of functional literacy and numeracy. We believe that for most people, functional literacy is equivalent to the achievement of Level 1 of the BSA standards, and that functional numeracy requires numeracy skills at Entry Level. Of course, adults above this functional level may have difficulties in certain contexts. However, once they achieve a functional level they reach a "take-off" point from which they should be able to access mainstream education or vocational training.

18 This definition is based on research that suggests that higher level literacy is required more often than higher level numeracy, both in everyday life[5] and in the workplace. For example, with respect to employment, research suggests that

5 *Basic Skills in Everyday Life*, The Basic Skills Agency, 1994

those with low and very low literacy become increasingly less likely to be in full-time employment than those with better skills. However, with respect to numeracy, it is only those with very low skills that are marked out as having particular difficulty in maintaining employment[6]. Research into the basic skills needed at work also shows that, whilst the average requirement for reading and writing skills is at Level 1, numeracy skills are required at about entry level.[7]

19 We recognise that in specific contexts, and in specific occupations, the level of skills required to function effectively will be higher. For example, in a number of occupations, it will be important to improve the numeracy of employees to Level 1 standard. Furthermore, in future, the skills required to be functional in work and society are likely to increase.

Level 2

20 At a number of points in the report we refer to skills at Level 2. By this we mean, broadly, the literacy or numeracy required to meet the standards of a key skills qualification at Level 2, or, very roughly, the underlying literacy/numeracy required to achieve GCSE grades A*-C. Though the achievement of Level 2 is not the focus of our report, a proportion of the adults improving their basic skills will rightly be aiming for Level 2 skills. This is why some of our recommendations relate to opportunities for these learners.

6 *It Doesn't Get any Better, Bynner and Parsons, The Basic Skills Agency, 1997*
7 *Basic Skills and Jobs, Institute for Employment Studies, The Basic Skills Agency, 1993*

Annex B – Evidence and Consultation

We are grateful to all those listed in this Annex who submitted evidence, or met with members of the Working Group.

1. Written evidence:

Adult Dyslexia Organisation
A J Baxter (dyslexia teacher)
A M Coward (Yeovil College)
A Pelleschi (Headteacher)
Anne Faloon (Leeds College of Technology)
Association of Colleges
B Mirzai (Adult Education teacher)
BE Consultancy
Bilston Community College
Bournemouth & Poole Further Education College
Bradford and Ilkley Community College
Bristol Youth Education Service
The British Chambers of Commerce
BBC Education
British Dyslexia Association
British Educational Communications and Technology agency (BECTa)
Calderdale College
Carlton Television
Channel 4 Television
City & Council of Swansea
City & Guilds
City and Islington College
The Community Self Build Agency (CSBA)
Core Skills Development Partnership, Birmingham
D Watford (Yeovil College)
Dearne Valley College
Debbie Cross (student)
Department of Health
Derbyshire County Council
Dorset Careers
Durham County Council
The Dyslexia Institute
Equal Opportunities Commission
Essential Skills Service, Yeovil College
Francis White
Further Education Development Agency
Geoff Kirkby (student)
Gloucestershire County Council Education Department
Greater Peterborough Chamber of Commerce, Training & Enterprise
Heather McKay (Edge Hill University College)
Highbury College, Portsmouth
Humberside Training and Enterprise Council
Independent Television Commission
Ingrid Thorstad
Institute of Education, University of London
Institute of Personnel and Development
Julie Matthews (student)
Keighley College
Kent Training and Enterprise Council
Lancashire Area West Training and Enterprise Council (LAWTEC)
The Learning Freeway, Havering Adult College
Lewisham College
Link into Learning, Cornwall
Literacy Research Group, Lancaster University
London Chamber of Commerce and Industry
London Language and Literacy Unit
Lorna Hayward (Adult Education/English for Speakers of Other Languages teacher)
Manchester Local Education Authority
Medway Council
Mid Essex Adult Community College
Mr F.H Waite (student)
National Association for Teaching English and Other Community Languages to Adults
National Association of Citizens Advice Bureaux
National Institute of Adult Continuing Education (NIACE)
NCH Action for Children
Newham Council
Nicola Beglin (part-time basic skills tutor)
Norfolk County Council Education Department
North and West Essex Community College
North East Lincolnshire Adult Education
North Lincolnshire Adult Education Service
Norwich City College
Oaklands College
PLANWEL (software training and development centre)
Read on – Write Away!, Derbyshire
Research and Practice in Adult Literacy (RAPAL)
Richard Hopkins (Phoenix Rising)
Rowley Regis College
S O'Dwyer
Sheffield College
Skill: National Bureau for Students with Disabilities
South Tyneside College

Southampton City College
Stockport English Language Service
Suffolk County Council Education Department
United Kingdom Reading Association
University of Hull
University of Lincolnshire & Humberside
Walsall College of Continuing Education
West Sussex County Council
Westminster Adult Education Service
Workers Educational Association

2.Oral evidence was provided by:

- Andrew Smith MP, Minister for Employment, Welfare to Work and Equal Opportunities, Department for Education and Employment
- The Further Education Funding Council
- The Training Standards Council
- OFSTED
- The Qualifications and Curriculum Authority
- The Local Government Association
- The TEC National Council
- Dr. Tom Sticht, President and Senior Scientist, Applied Behavioural and Cognitive Sciences, Inc., University of California

3. Members of the Group consulted the following individuals:

- Eileen Allen, Senior Education Officer, Independent Television Commission
- Nick Carey and colleagues, City & Guilds
- John Cridland, Conferation of British Industry
- Jane Drabble, Director of Education, BBC
- Ruth Spellman, Investors in People UK
- Moira Wallace, Jon Bright, Social Exclusion Unit

4.The following organisations attended feedback meetings:

- Association of Colleges
- BBC
- BECTa
- British Dyslexia Association
- Campaign for Learning
- Channel 4
- City & Guilds
- FEDA
- FEFC
- HM Prison Service, Education Services
- NIACE
- OFSTED
- QCA
- TEC National Council
- Training Standards Council

5.Learner Focus Groups

Four focus groups were held with adults on basic skills programmes in four areas of the country. The sites of the focus groups were chosen to reflect a range of programmes. Learners from the following programmes were consulted:

- Warrington Collegiate Institute
- Norfolk County Council
- Tower Hamlets College
- Maidstone prison

6.Expert Seminar

In July 1998 a seminar was held to gain the views of basic skills practitioners. The following individuals attended this seminar:

- Yasmin Akbar-Shah, Tower Hamlets College
- Maureen Beckwith, Havering Adult College
- Nadine Cartner, Association of Colleges
- Lorraine Collins, Hillingdon Adult Education Service
- Jay Derrick, City and Islington College
- Fiona Frank, Lancaster Employee Development Consortium
- Chris Hopwood, Wakefield College/National Support Project for FE Colleges
- Henry Kelly, South Tyneside College
- Ian Livingstone, Barnsley College
- Miriam Sampson, Highbury College, Portsmouth
- Sue Southwood, Ford Motor Company

Annex C – References

We found the following publications particularly helpful in writing this report:

A Official

i) Department for Education and Employment

Department for Education and Employment, *Adult and Community Learning Fund: Prospectus*, (DfEE, 1998)

Department for Education and Employment, *Excellence in Schools*, (DfEE, 1997)

Department for Education and Employment, *Further Education for the New Millennium*, (DfEE, 1998)

Department for Education and Employment, *The Learning Age: a renaissance for a new Britain*, (DfEE, 1998)

Department for Education and Employment, TECs: *Meeting the Challenge of the Millennium: Consultation Paper*, (DfEE, 1998)

Department for Education and Employment, *University for Industry: Engaging people in learning for life – Pathfinder Prospectus*, (DfEE, 1998)

Literacy Task Force, *The Implementation of the National Literacy Strategy*, (DfEE, 1997)

Numeracy Task Force, *Numeracy Matters: The Preliminary Report of the Numeracy Task Force*, (DfEE, 1998)

ii) Other

Department of the Environment, Transport and the Regions, *Building Partnerships for Prosperity: Sustainable Growth, Competititveness and Employment in the English Regions*, (DETR, 1997)

The Education and Training Action Group for Wales, *An Education and Training Action Plan for Wales: A Draft for Consultation*, (Manweb plc, 1998)

The Further Education Funding Council, *Basic Education: Curriculum Area Survey Report*, (FEFC, 1998)

House of Commons Select Committee on Education and Employment, *Sixth Report: Further Education*, (HMSO, 1998)

HM Prison Service, Education Services, *Focus on Education within Prisons: Briefing for All Party Parliamentary Group on Adult Education*, (HM Prison Service Regime Services, 1998)

Kennedy, H., *Learning Works: Widening participation in further education*, (FEFC, 1997)

National Advisory Council for Education and Training Targets, *National Learning Targets for England for 2002*, (DfEE, 1998)

National Advisory Group for Continuing Education and Lifelong Learning, *Learning for the Twenty-First Century*, (DfEE, 1997)

National Skills Task Force, *Towards a National Skills Agenda*, (DfEE, 1998)

Office for National Statistics, *Adult Literacy in Britain*, (ONS, 1997)

Office for Standards in Education, *The Annual Report of Her Majesty's Chief Inspector of Schools 1996/97*, (OFSTED, 1998)

Organisation for Economic Cooperation and Development / Human Resources Development Canada, *Literacy Skills for the Knowledge Society*, (OECD, 1997)

Qualifications and Curriculum Authority, *Literacy and Numeracy in the Workplace*, (QCA, 1997)

Qualifications and Curriculum Authority, *Implementation of the Dearing Review of Qualifications for 16-19 Year Olds*, (QCA, 1997)

Social Exclusion Unit, *Bringing Britain together: a national strategy for neighbourhood renewal*, (HMSO, 1998)

B Basic Skills Agency

ALBSU/Gallup, *The Cost to British Industry: Basic Skills and the Workforce*, (ALBSU, 1993)

ALBSU, *Parents and their Children*, (ALBSU, 1993)

The Basic Skills Agency, *Staying the Course*, (BSA, 1997)

The Basic Skills Agency, *Quality Standards for Basic Skills Programmes*, (BSA, 1997)

The Basic Skills Agency/National Foundation for Educational Research, *Family Numeracy Adds Up*, (BSA, 1998)

Bynner, J., and Parsons, S., It *Doesn't Get Any Better*, (BSA, 1997)

Bynner, J., and Parsons, S., *Does Numeracy Matter?*, (BSA, 1997)

Bynner, J., and Parsons, S., *Use It or Lose It?*, (BSA, 1998)

Bynner, J., and Parsons, S., *Influences on Adult Basic Skills* (BSA, 1998)

Carr-Hill, R., Passingham, S., Wolf, A., and Kent, N., *Lost Opportunities*, (BSA, 1995)

Ekinsmyth, C., and Bynner, J., *The Basic Skills of Young Adults*, (BSA, 1994)

Institute for Employment Studies, *Basic Skills and Jobs*, (ALBSU, 1993)

Kambouri, M., and Francis, H., *Time to Leave?: Progression and Drop Out in Basic Skills Programmes*, (ALBSU, 1994)

National Foundation for Educational Research, *Family Literacy Lasts*, (BSA, 1997)

WMEB Consultants and Ross, K., *Basic Skills Training at Work: A Study of Effectiveness*, (ALBSU, 1995)